D1538603

TRINITY CHURCH, NEWARK

HISTORIC ROADSIDES
IN NEW JERSEY

A Condensed Description of the
Principal Colonial and Revolutionary Landmarks in New Jersey,
arranged for the Convenience of
Students and Motorists.

The Society of Colonial Wars in the
State of New Jersey

1928

For Purchase of Copies Address
WALTER LESTER GLENNEY, ESQ., Secretary
916 Madison Avenue
Plainfield, N. J.

Press of Innes & Sons
Philadelphia

PREFACE

IN the foreword of "The First Americans" the Editors say, "The beginning of the thirteen English Colonies, so big with destiny, have stirred the reverent curiosity of American historians generation after generation." It is one of the objects of the Society of Colonial Wars to promote an interest in and knowledge of Colonial history, not only by historians but by the ordinary man who professes that he has no time to devote to things that are past.

In this day when distance is made unimportant by the motor vehicle, and we can in a day cover a mileage, which would have taken many days in Colonial times, there is no excuse for unfamiliarity or lack of knowledge of the historic spots in one's own State. When the State is one with a history so fascinating and so closely connected with our National history, there is even less excuse for ignorance. The location of Colonial settlements was determined in a great measure by nearness to river transportation. It is for this reason that we find New Jersey's beginnings at opposite ends of the Colony. New York Bay led to the settlements of the Dutch near Bergen and other points on the Hudson. Raritan Bay and river attracted the settlers from Connecticut, who founded Newark. In the South the Delaware Bay and the river navigable to Trenton, provided easy access for the settlements, made first by the Swedes and later by the Quakers.

In the Revolution New Jersey was the battle ground of the country and no part of the Colonies experienced more deeply the bitterness of the hatred between Tory and Continental. Fort Mercer, Trenton, Princeton, Toms River are a few of the glorious names in New Jersey's battle roll. They are truly a few, when we recall that within the present Union County there were eighteen battles or engagements between March, 1777, and June, 1781.

The honored Governor of the Society of Colonial Wars in the State of New Jersey, the Hon. Charles Lathrop Pack, who has made himself known nationally by his interest in and work for forest conservation, is equally interested in the preservation of the history of New Jersey and desiring to promote a wider knowledge of it on the part of the people of the State, has undertaken to provide for the publication by the Society of a Road Book of Historic New Jersey with the hope that the motorist or tourist may be able to make his travel or touring not only pleasant but profitable in the revival of a knowledge of the past history of our State.

The work of preparation of the Road Book was entrusted to the Junior Council of the Society and has been prosecuted to a completion, made possible by the generosity and co-operation of Governor Pack and some of his friends.

The thanks of the Council are due to the Rev. Arthur Adams, the learned Librarian of Trinity College, Hartford, Connecticut, a native of New Jersey and deeply versed in her history, for his reading and correction of the manuscript.

The historical map of New Jersey, published by Rand McNally Company, is used under an arrangement made with them by the compiler of the data, by which the right to use the map was reserved for the benefit of the Society of Colonial Wars in the State of New Jersey.

By the courtesy of Wm. H. Broadwell, of Newark, New Jersey, a member of the Newark Chapter, S. A. R., and Newark Historical Society, the Committee have been enabled to make use, in this book, of many beautiful photographs taken by him.

In issuing this booklet, which it is hoped will find its way into the public schools, it is too much to hope that it is free from error or that we have not omitted some spot which should be included. If errors or omissions be found, they can be corrected in future editions. Dr. Andrews in "The Colonial Background of the American Revolution," says, "A nation's attitude towards its own history is like a window into its own soul." In sending out this booklet we adopt this view and shall hope that its reception and use will show that within, the New Jerseyman is proud of his State and its past.

HISTORICAL COMMITTEE

JAMES M. CROWELL   CHARLES M. JONES
TENNILLE DIX   FRANK W. MELVIN
WALTER L. GLENNEY   WALTER MOSES
DR. D. WEBB GRANBERRY   J. BROOKS B. PARKER
E. BURD GRUBB   GEORGE VAN W. VOORHEES
REV. H. ST. CLAIR HATHAWAY JOHN V. B. WICOFF
               FRANCIS CHAPMAN, *Chairman*

MAY 1, 1928

NEW JERSEY, containing a total area of eight thousand two hundred and twenty-four square miles, has an extreme length north and south of one hundred and sixty-six miles and an extreme width east and west of fifty-seven miles. Within this small area has been crowded some of the most important events in the history of our land. It is, therefore, fitting to note something of the history of the State.

The first authenticated visit of any European to what is now the State of New Jersey was made under French authority by da Verazano, a Florentine, who, in the Spring of 1524, dropped anchor within Sandy Hook. In 1614, Cornelius Jacobsen Mey, explored the lower Delaware. In 1623 Mey built Fort Nassau on the eastern bank of the Delaware River near the present site of Gloucester City. In 1631 Godyn and Blommaert secured a patent from Peter Minuit, authorizing the planning of a settlement near Cape May. In 1633 a trading hut was established at Paulus Hook, near the present site of Jersey City and another trading post was later established on the west bank of the Hudson on the site of Hoboken.

In 1641 a Colony from New Haven attempted a settlement on Salem Creek, but Swedes and Dutch united and jointly attacked and burned the place. About 1643 the Swedes constructed a triangular fort called Elfsborg, on the eastern bank of the Delaware, near the present town of Salem. The Fort, because of the great number of mosquitos, was abandoned and called in derision, the "Mosquito Fort."

In 1655 Peter Stuyvesant put an end to Swedish rule in New Jersey and retained control until 1664, when Sir Robert Carr, in command of the British, took possession of the settlements on the Delaware. While the expedition of Nicholls and Carr was still at sea, the Duke of York granted to Lord John Berkley and Sir George Carteret that part of the New Netherland between the Hudson and Delaware Rivers. To this tract, the name Nova Caesarea or New Jersey was given in honor of Carteret, who, in 1649, had defended the Isle of Jersey.

The settlements in the Colony were Bergen on the west shore of Newark Bay and the settlements of the Swedes and Dutch in Gloucester and Burlington Counties. At Long Point on the Delaware, now the site of Burlington, there were three Dutch families. In 1665, Philip Carteret arrived at Elizabeth-town, commissioned as Governor of the Province. Shrewsbury and Middletown claiming to hold under grants from Governor Nicholls, refused to take part in the Colonial Assembly and their delegates were expelled. The first Colonial Assembly was held May 26, 1668, at Elizabeth.

March 18, 1673, Lord Berkley sold his interest to John Fenwick, a former Major in the Parliamentary Army and to Edward Byllynge, both of whom were Quakers. The original line between the portion of the Province held by Carteret and that sold to Fenwick and Byllynge was drawn from Barnegat Creek to Rankokuskill, a small stream south of Burlington. Fenwick and Byllynge, having disagreed, referred their matter to William Penn for arbitration. He awarded to Byllynge nine-tenths of the territory and to Fenwick one-tenth. Subsequently Byllynge assigned his nine-tenths in trust for creditors to William Penn, Gawen Lawrie and Lucas, who latter acquired the share of Fenwick as well. In 1675 Fenwick came to Salem in the Ship Griffin of London. In 1676 the interest of Carteret, Penn, Lawrie, Lucas and Byllynge were determined by a line drawn from Little Egg Harbor on the Atlantic to a point on the Delaware River 41° 40′ north latitude, and that portion east of the line or East Jersey was assigned to Carteret, the west or West Jersey to the Quaker Associates.

In August, 1677, the Ship Kent arrived, bringing two hundred and thirty Quakers from London and Yorkshire, who founded a settlement first called New Beverley, but finally

Burlington. In 1678 the Ship Shield from Hull brought further Colonists.

The years 1678 to 1680 were taken up with quarrels between Sir Edmund Andros, Governor of New York, and Carteret. In 1681 the controversy was referred to Sir William Jones in England for adjudication, who decided against Andros. In November of the same year, Samuel Jennings, Governor, convened the West Jersey Assembly at Burlington. In February, 1682, Penn and his followers purchased East Jersey for the sum of thirty-four hundred pounds and the Duke of York issued a patent in March, 1683.

In 1682 the Colony of East Jersey was divided into four Counties, Bergen, Essex, Middlesex and Monmouth. It continued to grow under the various Colonial Governors Rudyard, Lawrie and Lord Neill Campbell, until 1702, when Lord Cornbury became Governor. The seven years of his administration were marked by strife and confusion. He was succeeded by John, Lord Lovelace, and he in turn by Robert Hunter, Governor for nine years, for whom Hunterdon County is named. William Burnet, son of Bishop Burnet, served from 1719 to 1726; John Montgomerie, five years, 1726 to 1731; Lewis Morris, 1738 to 1746; and Jonathan Belcher, 1747 to 1757. William Franklin, the last Royal Governor of New Jersey, administered the affairs of the Province from 1762 to 1776. On the 26th of May, 1776, the second Provincial Congress met at Burlington, Trenton, and New Brunswick. By its orders Governor Franklin was arrested and deported, remaining a prisoner for two years. William Livingston became Governor in 1776 and held the office till 1790.

On September 20, 1777, the Legislature of the Colony struck out the word "Colony" and substituted the word "State" in its organic law. In 1786 it sent delegates to the Annapolis Convention and later to the Constitutional Convention. The Federal Constitution was ratified by unanimous vote December 18, 1787.

GOVERNORS OF NEW JERSEY

Governors under the Proprietors

PHILIP CARTERET..1665-1672
JOHN BERRY 1672-1673
ANTHONY COLVE...1673-1674

Governors of East Jersey and their Deputies

PHILIP CARTERET..1674-1682
ROBERT BARCLAY 1682-1688
THOMAS RUDYARD, Deputy....................................1682-1683
GAWEN LAWRIE, Deputy......................................1683-1686
LORD NEILL CAMPBELL, Deputy...............................1686-1687
ANDREW HAMILTON, Deputy...................................1687-1690
EDMUND ANDROS...1688-1689
ANDREW HAMILTON 1692-1697
JEREMIAH BASSE..1698-1699
ANDREW HAMILTON 1699-1702

Governors of West Jersey and their Deputies

EDWARD BYLLYNGE 1680-1687
SAMUEL JENNINGS, Deputy...................................1681-1684
THOMAS OLIVE, Deputy......................................1684-1685
JOHN SKENE, Deputy 1685-1687
DANIEL COX...1687-1688
EDMOND ANDROS 1688-1689
EDWARD HUNLOKE, Deputy.................................... 1690
ANDREW HAMILTON 1692-1697
JEREMIAH BASSE 1697-1699
ANDREW HAMILTON 1699-1702

UNDER THE ROYAL GOVERNMENT

Governors of New Jersey and New York

EDWARD HYDE, Lord Cornbury................................1703-1708
JOHN, Lord Lovelace 1708-1709
RICHARD INGOLDSBY, Lieut. and Governor...................1709-1710
ROBERT HUNTER 1710-1719
WILLIAM BURNET 1720-1728

JOHN MONTGOMERIE.....................................1728-1731
LEWIS MORRIS, President of Council....................1731-1732
WILLIAM COSBY 1732-1736
JOHN ANDERSON, President of Council.................. 1736
JOHN HAMILTON, President of Council..................1736-1738

Governors of New Jersey Only

LEWIS MORRIS 1738-1746
JOHN HAMILTON, President of Council..................1746-1747
JOHN READING, President of Council................... 1747
JONATHAN BELCHER 1747-1757
THOMAS POWNALL, Lieut. Governor 1757
JOHN READING, President of Council...................1757-1758
FRANCIS BERNARD 1758-1760
THOMAS BOONE 1760-1761
JOSIAH HARDY 1761-1762
WILLIAM FRANKLIN 1763-1776

Governors of the State

WILLIAM LIVINGSTON 1776-1790
WILLIAM PATERSON 1790-1792
RICHARD HOWELL 1792-1801
JOSEPH BLOOMFIELD 1801-1802
JOHN LAMBERT (Acting) 1802-1803
JOSEPH BLOOMFIELD 1803-1812
AARON OGDEN.......................................1812-1813
WILLIAM SANDFORD PENNINGTON......................1813-1815
MAHLON DICKERSON 1815-1817
ISAAC HALSTED WILLIAMSON...........................1817-1829
GARRET DORSET WALL (Declined).................... 1829
PETER DUMONT VROOM..............................1829-1832
SAMUEL LEWIS SOUTHARD............................1832-1833
ELIAS P. SEELY..................................... 1833
PETER DUMONT VROOM..............................1833-1836
PHILEMON DICKINSON 1836-1837
WILLIAM PENNINGTON 1837-1843
DANIEL HAINES 1843-1844
CHARLES C. STRATTON...............................1845-1848
DANIEL HAINES 1848-1851

[8]

GEORGE FRANKLIN FORT................................1851-1854
RODMAN MCCAULEY PRICE..............................1854-1857
WILLIAM AUGUSTUS NEWELL..........................1857-1860
CHARLES SMITH OLDEN 1860-1863
JOEL PARKER 1863-1866
MARCUS LAWRENCE WARD.............................1866-1869
THEODORE FRELINGHUYSEN RANDOLPH 1869-1872
JOEL PARKER 1872-1875
JOSEPH DORSETT BEDLE...............................1875-1878
GEORGE BRINTON MCCLELLAN.........................1878-1881
GEORGE CRAIG LUDLOW...............................1881-1884
LEON ABBETT 1884-1887
ROBERT STOCKTON GREEN.............................1887-1890
LEON ABBETT 1890-1893
GEORGE THEODORE WERTS.............................1893-1896
JOHN WILLIAM GRIGGS...............................1896-1898
FOSTER MACGOWAN VOORHEES (Acting)................. 1898
DAVID O. WATKINS..................................1898-1899
FOSTER MACGOWAN VOORHEES.........................1899-1902
FRANKLIN MURPHY 1902-1905
EDWARD CASPER STOKES..............................1905-1908
JOHN FRANKLIN FORT................................1908-1911
WOODROW WILSON 1911-1913
JAMES F. FIELDER, Acting Governor..................... 1913
LEON R. TAYLOR, Acting Governor....................1913-1914
JAMES F. FIELDER...................................1914-1917
WALTER E. EDGE....................................1917-1919
WILLIAM N. RUNYON, Acting Governor.................1919-1920
CLARENCE E. CASE, Acting Governor................... 1920
EDWARD I. EDWARDS................................1920-1923
GEORGE S. SILZER...................................1923-1926
A. HARRY MOORE.................................... 1926

ATLANTIC COUNTY

Atlantic County was organized in 1837 out of the eastern portion of Gloucester County. Bounded on north by Great Bay and Burlington County, on northwest by Camden and Gloucester Counties, southwest and south by Cumberland and Cape May Counties.

The region first appears in history about 1609, when Henry Hudson sailed the Half Moon to Absegani (Absecon Beach) and Eyre Haven or Egg Harbor, so named on account of the number of gulls' eggs found there. The original owner of Absecon Island was Thomas Budd, 1695. There were no permanent residents on Absecon Beach until about the time of the Revolution. Settlers from Long Island located near Somers Point as early as 1695.

In September, 1765, the ship Faithful Steward, carrying Stamp Act paper, came ashore on Absecon Beach and was wrecked. The passengers, trying to get ashore, were swamped and lost.

MAYS LANDING. County seat. It was originally a part of Hamilton Township. First settled in 1710 by George May. At one time a thriving port and ship-building center.

PLEASANT MILLS on Mullica River. The Richards Mansion located on the Sweetwater Creek close to Pleasant Mills, is the Aylesford Hall, home of Kate Aylesford, the fictitious heroine of Peterson's novel of that name. Tablet erected by Kate Aylesford Chapter, D. A. R., November 21, 1914, in memory of Revolutionary Soldiers buried here.

CHESTNUT NECK, on Mullica River. Once a thriving town carrying on a brisk trade in the Revolution; its boats going into Great Bay would seize British supply vessels and send the captured supplies to the American Army. In September, 1778, a British force of 9 vessels and 400 men was dispatched to destroy the place. Count Pulaski and his legion sent by Washington to relieve the town did not arrive in time. October 6, 1778, the British captured the Fort, destroyed all of the vessels in the harbor, pillaged, and burned the town. The scene of the engagement between Pulaski and his legion and the British across the Mullica River in Burlington County, is marked by a tablet erected by the Society of the Cincinnati in New Jersey. The Battle of Chestnut Neck is commemorated by a monument dedicated October 6, 1911, erected through an appropriation obtained by the General Lafayette Chapter, D. A. R., of Atlantic City, N. J.

SOMERS POINT. On Great Egg Harbor Bay, settled about 1693 by John Somers. Birthplace about 1778 of Richard Somers, who, in 1803, a Naval Lieutenant, commanded the Nautilus, a twelve gun schooner attached to the Mediterranean Squadron under Preble. He distinguished himself in the block-ade of Tripoli and is said to have originated the plan of destroy-ing the Tripolitan Fleet by a fire-ship. He commanded the fire-ship and lost his life in the explosion which destroyed her.

WEYMOUTH. Located on the river about six miles north-west of Mays Landing, is made interesting by the ruins of the Weymouth Foundry, built in the Eighteenth Century. The neighboring bogs contained iron, which at the foundry was con-verted into flint locks and cannon. Barber & Howe, in their historical collections of the State of New Jersey, state that in 1844 Weymouth contained a furnace, forge, saw and grist mill and about forty dwellings, the works belonging to the heirs of Samuel Richards and giving employment at the time to several hundred men.

BERGEN COUNTY

Bergen County, created in December, 1682, by Act of Assembly of East Jersey, dividing the province into the four counties of Bergen, Essex, Middlesex and Monmouth. The

County was enlarged by Act of January 21, 1709, having originally consisted only of a narrow strip five or six miles wide between Hackensack River and Hudson River. It is now bounded on the north by New York State, on the west by Passaic and Essex Counties, on the south by Hudson County, and on the east by the Hudson River. Passaic County was partly carved out of Bergen County in 1837, and Hudson County was taken from Bergen County in 1840.

FORT LEE. A small village on the Hudson, about five miles southeast of Hackensack. The Fort was three hundred feet above the river. Fort Lee was, in 1776, the site of a Fort, which, with Fort Washington on the east side of the Hudson River, was supposed to command the river. When Fort Washington was taken by the British November 16, 1776, it was necessary for the Continentals to evacuate Fort Lee, which was done November 20, 1776. General Greene commanded the retreating troops, crossing the Hackensack River north of Hackensack at Old Bridge, later known as New Bridge, and more recently as River Edge. The site of the old bridge has been located.

BULLS FERRY. A few miles below Fort Lee, where a ferry existed for more than a half century, the site of a small block-house held by the British. General Anthony Wayne made an unsuccessful attempt, July 20, 1780, to storm the block-house. The tradition is that the British defenders of the block-house had but a single round of ammunition left when the assault was given up.

NEW BARBADOES. Site of Tory attacks in 1779.

ARCOLA. Here lived Peter Lutkins, at whose home Washington slept on one occasion.

WEST ENGLEWOOD. The Liberty Pole is the third which has stood upon this site, the first being a tree from which floated the American Flag during the entire Revolutionary War, the present pole being erected by the Society of the Daughters of the Revolution of Englewood.

Hohokus. On road from Hackensack to Suffern. Here resided Colonel Provost, first husband of Madam Jumel, who later married Aaron Burr.

THE HERMITAGE, HOHOKUS

Hackensack. County Seat of Bergen County on west bank of Hackensack River. The town is ancient. The first building of the Dutch Church erected in 1696. In and near Hackensack repeated conflicts occurred between the British, Hessians and Refugees and the Continentals and Patriots. In September, 1777, Lieutenant Colonel Aaron Burr surprised the British Picket Guard at Hackensack and dispersed them after killing a considerable number. The following day the British abandoned the place. The stone Academy, presided over by Peter Wilson, LL.D., a Scotchman, was erected in 1762. Wilson was subsequently Professor of Languages at Columbia College and is buried near the grave of Brigadier General Enoch Poor in the graveyard of the First Reformed Dutch Church.

A monument to the memory of Brigadier General Enoch Poor was erected opposite the Court House. Poor, a Brigadier General of the State of New Hampshire, under the command of Lafayette, died September 8, 1780. Lafayette visited his grave in 1824.

The "Mansion House" was formerly the residence of Peter Zabriskie, where General Washington made his headquarters in 1776. Built in 1751. Became a tavern known as Albany Stage Coach. The tap room was occupied in 1825 by the Weehawken Bank. Room 19 is the traditional room occupied by George Washington. Marked by bronze tablet erected by Bergen County Historical Society.

CLOSTER. Above Huyler's Landing on the Hudson River. Raided by the Refugees July 10, 1779. Captain Harring and Thomas Branch, with a few of the neighbors hastily collected, attacked the Refugees, and took prisoners. To escape, the Refugees cut the cable of their vessel and let it drift with the tide, staying below decks.

BURLINGTON COUNTY

The boundaries of Burlington County were established in 1694, but not definitely settled until 1710, when Hunterdon County was organized, the Assunpink Creek being then made the boundary. In 1838 Burlington County was reduced by the organization of Mercer County and subsequently further reduced by the organization of the present Ocean County.

BURLINGTON. Founded in 1677 by Friends from Yorkshire and London under "The Concessions and Agreements of the Proprietors, Freeholders and Inhabitants of West Jersey in America." All vessels coming to West Jersey were required to enter and clear at the Port of Burlington. Provincial Capital, till 1755 and again from 1757 to 1790. The Provincial Congress of New Jersey met at Burlington in 1776 and elected the delegates to the Continental Congress who signed the

OLD ST. MARY'S CHURCH, BURLINGTON
Built 1703

Declaration of Independence. Town occupied by British for a few hours in December of 1776. Cannonaded by British from River, May 1778.

Points of interest:

1. St. Mary's P. E. Church founded and building erected 1703, chartered as St. Anne's October 4, 1704. By second charter, name was changed in 1709 to St. Mary's. Rev. Jonathan Odell, a grandson of Jonathan Dickinson, first President of Princeton, was Rector from 1767 to 1777. A Tory, he was arrested by the Continentals. He was concealed for a time at home of Margaret Morris, Green Bank. Noted for his fierce satires on America. Died in Nova Scotia. Communion Service of Church presented by Queen Anne.

2. Graveyard of St. Mary's Church. Graves of Elias Boudinot, first President of the American Bible Society and William Bradford, Attorney General of the United States under President Washington.

3. 457 S. High Street. Birthplace of J. Fenimore Cooper, 1789. Now home of Burlington County Historical Society.

4. 457 S. High Street. Home of Captain James Lawrence, 1781 to 1813.

5. 435 S. High Street. Home of Stephen Sallet.

6. High and Library Streets. Residence of Governor Bloomfield, soldier in the Revolution, Governor of New Jersey, Mayor of Burlington, and Grand Master of the Masons.

7. High Street above Broad Street. Alcazar Hotel. Residence of Thomas Olive who arrived on Ship Kent in 1677. Acting Governor of New Jersey in the absence of Samuel Jennings.

8. Blue Anchor Tavern, now Metropolitan Inn, built in 1751. At one time meeting place of West Jersey Proprietors.

9. Site of Court House, 1683. Center of Broad and High Streets. Court removed to Mt. Holly, 1796.

10. Site of Town Hall, 1794. Intersection of High and Union Streets. Council Chambers on second floor, prison in basement, whipping post in front.

11. 208 High Street. Office of Samuel Jennings. First Colonial money printed here 1726, by Benjamin Franklin.

12. 222 High Street. Residence of Thomas Gardner, Land Commissioner, built 1680. First Annual Meeting of Friends here 1683. Friends built a meeting house, hexagonal in shape, 1683. Present meeting house constructed 1784.

REVEL HOUSE—OLDEST IN BURLINGTON

13. East Pearl Street. Office of Thomas Revel, Registrar of New Jersey Proprietors, built 1685, now occupied by Annis Stockton Chapter, D. A. R.

14. Hickory Grove. Salem Road or Kings Highway, dwelling of Samuel Smith, Historian, and Samuel J. Smith, Poet.

15. Site of First School House. Northwest corner Broad and St. Mary Streets, now occupied by St. Barnabas Church.

16. Site of First House built in limits of Burlington, now farm of Robert Sutton, River Road.

17. Mantinicunk Island, once occupied by Peter Jegau, a Dutchman. By Act of Assembly the revenue derived from the island was devoted to maintaining public schools in Burlington.

18. Hessian Camp Ground, South High Street, occupied in 1776.

19. Yorkshire Bridge, East Broad Street, over the stream which made Burlington an island in Colonial times.

20. Friends Meeting House. High Street. Organized 1678.

21. Kinsey House. Home of James Kinsey, delegate to Continental Congress.

22. Ferry Slip. 1713. The first steam ferry boat, 1834.

23. Residence of Isaac Collins. Northeast corner York and Broad Streets. King's printer.

24. 135 W. Broad Street. Bradford House. Home of Elias Boudinot, President of the Continental Congress, 1782, director of Mint. Daughter married William Bradford, Attorney General under Washington.

GREEN BANK. Residence of Governor William Franklin. Later home of Margaret Morris who concealed Rev. Jonathan Odell, the Tory Rector. One time residence of E. Burd Grubb.

2. Sycamore Tree. Green Bank. To this tree, Ship Shield, first vessel bringing English Settlers so far up the Delaware, tied up in 1678. Site of landing marked by tablet, erected by Society of Colonial Wars in the State of New Jersey.

3. St. Mary's Hall. Green Bank. Oldest Church School for girls in the United States.

JACKSONVILLE. Small town outside of Burlington. Scene

of skirmish between British and American Troops. Blood stains from wounded soldiers still shown at church.

BEVERLY. The site of Dunk's Ferry, at the foot of Laurel Street. One detachment of Washington's Army was to have crossed the Delaware at Beverly over Dunk's Ferry and advance to Trenton from the south but was prevented from crossing by ice in the river. During the Civil War a recruiting camp and hospital were maintained at Beverly, and a National Cemetery on the outskirts of the place still exists.

BORDENTOWN. Settled in 1681 by Thomas Farnsworth. Takes its name from Joseph Borden, an early settler. In May, 1778, it was partly destroyed by the British, who had sent an expedition to destroy the vessels in Barnes and Crosswicks Creeks. The town is worthy of note for the names of illustrious residents, including Francis Hopkinson, J. Fenimore Cooper, Clara Barton, Richard Watson Gilder, Patience Wright, Admiral Charles Stewart, Joseph Bonaparte, once King of Spain, Prince Lucien Murat, and the daughters of Joseph Bonaparte.

Places of historical interest are:

1. Clara Barton's School. Built 1739, containing her desk, chair and pupil's chair. Building now owned and maintained by Red Cross.

2. Home of Richard Watson Gilder directly opposite Barton School, now given to Bordentown by the owner and dedicated to public use.

3. Farnsworth and Park Streets. Northwest corner. Home of Colonel Joseph Borden, son of Joseph Borden, who laid out the town. Original house burned by the British during the Revolution. Colonel Borden returning from the War built house now standing, retaining original iron railing.

4. Northeast corner Park and Farnsworth Streets, once the American Hotel.

5. Southwest corner. Home of Patience Wright, first American Sculptress, who, after the Revolution, went to England.

6. Southeast corner. Home of Judge Harold B. Wells, formerly home of Francis Hopkinson, Poet, Signer of the Declaration of Independence and Chairman of Committee designing American Flag. Father of Joseph Hopkinson, author of "Hail Columbia." Francis Hopkinson was author of "The Battle of the Kegs." Tablet erected in his memory by Francis Hopkinson Chapter D. A. R., October 22, 1921.

7. Point Breeze, Park Street. Residence of Joseph Bonaparte.

8. On the River Bank, Industrial School, main building of which was formerly home of Admiral Charles Stewart of American Navy, grandfather of Charles Stewart Parnell.

CROSSWICKS. Four miles east of Bordentown. Settled in 1681. Scene of a skirmish in June, 1778, between the Continental Troops and a detachment of the British Army retreating from Philadelphia to New York via Bordentown and Monmouth. The contest occurred at the bridge over Crosswicks Creek, the Continentals endeavoring to destroy the bridge and prevent the crossing. During the skirmish, a cannon ball fired struck the Old Friends Meeting House at Crosswicks, which still bears the marks of the shot, the ball being kept as a curiosity.

MOORESTOWN. Nine miles from Mt. Holly and nine miles from Camden. Derived its name from an early settler named Moore and was settled at an early date. Scene of a British encampment on the night of June 19, 1778, on land now owned by Amos Stiles and Benjamin Warrington, about three hundred yards from the Friends Meeting House.

Home of Commodore Truxton, distinguished American Naval Commander, located on road from Moorestown to Mt. Holly about one and a half miles from Moorestown.

CROSSWICKS MEETING HOUSE
Bearing Marks of Cannon Shot, June 23, 1778

Mt. Holly. Settled by the Friends not long after the settlement of Burlington, originally known as Bridgeton. Of considerable importance in Revolutionary War. Legislature of New Jersey held some of its meetings here and British Troops were quartered on the inhabitants. William, Duke of Clarence, later King William IV, was stationed there with the British Troops in the Revolution.

Places of note:

1. Residence of Stephen Girard. Mill Street.

2. Court House erected 1796.

3. Friends Meeting House built 1775, occupied by British as Commissary Department, also used for sessions of State Legislature during Revolution.

4. Brainerd's School House used by the British as a stable.

5. Brainerd's Presbyterian Church used by British for stable and burned on leaving town.

6. On road from Mt. Holly to Springfield, residence of John Woolman, 1720 to 1772, author of Woolman's Journal and first Preacher of abolition of slavery. Residence is still in existence and is now a tea-room.

Mt. Holly, home of William Denning, maker of first wrought-iron cannon made in the world, one of which was completed prior to Battle of the Brandywine and captured by the British. Denning refused British offers of an annuity and sums of money to instruct them in the manufacture of guns.

Mt. Holly was, in 1757, site of a draft for soldiers to be sent to relief of Fort William Henry, then infested by French and Indians.

BATSTO. About twenty-eight miles southeast of Mt. Holly on Batsto River, in Washington Township. Batsto was founded in 1766 by Charles Reed. During Revolution, site of an iron furnace owned by Colonel John Cox, employed in casting cannon shot and bomb shells for the American Army.

HOME OF JOHN WOOLMAN, MT. HOLLY

CAMDEN COUNTY

Camden County, originally part of old Gloucester, was organized under an Act passed by the Legislature March 13, 1844. Long-a-Coming (Berlin) was the first County Seat, but in 1848 at a fourth election held to vote on a County Seat, Camden won a majority and is now the seat of the county government. The County was named, as is the City, after Charles Pratt, Earl of Camden, a great Judge, a wise Statesman and warm advocate of fair play for the Colonies. The County is bounded on the northeast by Burlington; on the southeast by Atlantic; on the southwest by Gloucester and on the northwest by the Delaware River.

CAMDEN, originally styled "Pyne Poynte" and later Cooper's Ferry, was settled in 1681 by Richard Arnold and William Cooper, who built on the River's edge below the mouth of Deer Creek. He had a deed from the Proprietors of West Jersey, but also bought the land from the Indians, obtaining a deed executed by Tolacca, Chief of the Tribe. His second house was above Cooper's Point called by him Pyne Point, and is still standing. A ferry to Philadelphia was established near the foot of Cooper Street by the County and a license to operate it was granted to William Royden. It was bought from Royden by Cooper and the settlement became known as Cooper's Ferry. The ferry over Cooper's Creek was established, at what is now Federal Street, in 1747 by Samuel Spicer.

Kaighn's Point, was settled by John Kaighn in 1696, and land lower down the River was bought by Archibald Mickle, who, with Cooper and Kaighn, owned practically all of Camden between Cooper's Creek and the Delaware.

In February of 1778, General Wayne forced the British to take shelter behind the works at Cooper's Point and on March 1, 1778, a spirited skirmish took place between Sixth and Market Streets and Cooper's Creek Bridge, Count Pulaski distinguishing himself.

In June of 1777, the Trustees of Princeton College held a meeting at Cooper's Ferry and granted degrees to the Class of '76, the only meeting of the Trustees held out of Princeton because of the War.

The first Charter was granted to Camden in 1828. The Camden and Amboy Railroad was chartered in 1830, and the first train ran into Camden January, 1834.

Points of interest:

1. 1128-30 S. Second Street. Southeast corner of Second and Sycamore Streets. House of John Kaighn, founder of Kaighn's Point.

2. Point Street House. At head of Point Street, bearing date 1734, headquarters of General Abercrombie, British Commander in the Revolution.

3. Cooper Park. Elm tree grown from a sucker from the Penn Treaty Elm in Philadelphia.

4. Mt. Ephraim Avenue and Mt. Vernon Street. Friends Meeting House built 1801.

5. Champion Road. West Collingswood Railroad Station site of home of Mark Newbie, authorized by Act of Assembly of 1682 to circulate "Mark Newbie's half pence," also called "Patrick's half pence," on giving security for redemption.

6. South side of Cooper Street, near Friends Avenue, site of home of the Naturalist, John James Audubon.

7. 328 Mickle Street. Home of Walt Whitman.

8. Harleigh Cemetery. Tomb of Walt Whitman.

9. Cooper House at Pyne Poynte.

HADDONFIELD. On Cooper's Creek about five miles southeast of Camden. The place takes its name from the family of John Haddon, who purchased the land on which the town is built about 1710. His daughter, Elizabeth Haddon, came to New Jersey from England and built a brick residence about 1713, later referred to. Haddonfield, although inhabited by Quakers, was successively occupied by American and British Troops and was the scene of a number of skirmishes.

Points of interest:

1. The Indian King Tavern. Built 1750. Meeting place of State Legislature in 1777, where the great Seal of the State was received and adopted. Building owned by State and managed by a commission. Marked by a tablet erected by Daughters of American Revolution.

2. Opposite Indian King, on Kings Highway, is the building used as a guard-house during Revolution. This guardhouse was on the premises of William Griscomb.

3. Kings Highway and Haddon Avenue. Buttonwood trees dating to the Revolution marked by tablet.

BUTTONWOOD TREE, HADDONFIELD

THE INDIAN KING TAVERN, HADDONFIELD

4. Friends Meeting House first built 1720. Present meeting house built 1760 on same site.

5. Estaugh. Site of house of Elizabeth Haddon on road to Camden. Present house built 1842 on foundation of original house. The still or brew house of Elizabeth Haddon still exists, also a yew tree brought from England in 1713 and a box hedge. On the present house, on the side door, is to be found the brass knocker of the original house of Elizabeth Haddon.

6. Memory of Elizabeth Haddon commemorated by tablet placed on buttonwood tree in Orthodox Friends Graveyard.

CAPE MAY COUNTY

Cape May was discovered by Sir Henry Hudson in The Half Moon August 28, 1609. He entered Delaware Bay, subsequently called South Bay and anchored a few miles north of Cape May Point, spending a day in exploring the Cape. The original Indian Settlers were called Kechemeches. The Delaware River was called Whittuck and what is now New Jersey was Skaakbee or Sheyichbi. Tuckahoe appears to be the only Indian name surviving in the County.

Cape May County and Cape were named from Cornelius Jacobsen Mey, who, in 1621, was sent by the Dutch West India Company in the Good Tidings and explored the coast.

On May 5, 1630, Samuel Godyn and Samuel Blommaert, exploring for the Dutch West India Company, purchased of the Indians a tract of land extending four miles along the Bay from Cape May Point northward and four miles inland. The deed, recorded on June 3, 1631, is still preserved among the Colonial records of the State and is the first in the County.

In 1631 David Pieterson de Vries, an eminent Dutch navigator, became the first resident Patroon owner in Cape May where he engaged in whaling. In 1641, Cape May and nearly all the Bay Shore north of it, were purchased from the Indians by Swedish agents.

The first settlement of importance was at New England Town, also called Town Bank and Cape May Town, about 1685, by whalers from Cape Cod and Southampton, Long Island.

In a letter dated 1688, Dr. Coxe speaks of having helped to plant a town at an expense of three thousand pounds for the development of the whaling industry. This settlement, in addition to names given above, is referred to in the early records as Portsmouth and as Falmouth. The New England settlers brought old names with them and it is notable that one of the founders of New England Town was Captain Ezekial Eldridge, who came from Falmouth on Cape Cod.

The site of this village on the Bay Shore about four miles north of the Point, was washed away by the sea prior to the Revolution. Some of the settlers, notably Hannah Gorham Whillden, were children or grandchildren of certain Pilgrim settlers of Plymouth Colony. Their descendants, together with those of Joseph Whillden, Thomas Leaming, Humphrey Hughes, Cornelius Schellinger, Samuel Crowell, Thomas Hand, and Ezekial Eldridge, are still to be found in the County.

New England Town where the first County Court was held in 1693, was abandoned prior to the Revolution because of the cessation of the whaling industry and because of the more permanent settlement, which after 1690 grew up at Cape Island, the present Cape May City. On May 10, 1692, at the house of Benjamin Godfrey was held the first Town Meeting in the County, and the first County Court appears to have been held here June 16, 1694.

An interesting experiment was attempted by Dr. Daniel Coxe, who had been physician to the Queen of Charles II, and to Anne, subsequently Queen. He acquired proprietary rights in 1688 to 95,000 acres, the larger portion of the County, and built Coxehall as a centre for a proprietary or manorial system of government. This existed from 1690 to 1692, when Dr. Coxe broke up his holdings. The first map of the County based on survey, appears to have been made by Lewis Morris in 1706, and the first road giving land connections to the north, through the Cedar Swamps, was completed in 1707.

The County was first organized in 1692 and its limits definitely determined in 1710.

DENNISVILLE. On entering the County, on the south side of Dennis Creek, is Dennisville. Founded in 1726 by Anthony Ludlam.

CAPE MAY COURT HOUSE. Surveyed and laid out in 1703 by Jeremiah Hand. First called Rumney Marsh and afterward Middleton.

Points of interest:

1. Site of first Court House and jail. Court first met in private houses and in First Baptist Church. In 1764, Daniel Hand, grandson of Shamgar Hand, one of the pioneer settlers, gave one acre as a site for a Court House and jail, which were built at the cost of three hundred pounds and continued in use until 1849, when it was re-placed by the present structure.

2. First Baptist Church. Baptist Meetings were held at New England Town and at Coxehall prior to 1690. This de-nomination claims that its first religious meetings were held as early as 1675, disputing priority with Cold Spring Presbyterian Church. It is certain that a nucleus of Bap-tists associated with the Baptist Church in Philadelphia existed prior to the formal organizing of the present church in 1712.

In 1741 a brick church was erected on the present site and was used until burned in 1854. The cemetery, which is adjacent, contains the graves of many original pioneers and of their descendants. The most notable is the grave of Aaron Leaming, who died August 22, 1780, leaving an estate of one hundred and eighty-one thousand pounds. He had served his County thirty years in the Assembly and his diary, together with the diary of Jacob Spicer, is the chief source of Colonial information for the County.

EARLY FRIENDS' MEETING HOUSE. On road from Court House to Seaville, just before reaching the latter place. Meeting organized about 1700 by the Leaming and Townsend families. Meeting House built in 1716 is well preserved.

COLD SPRING. Cold Spring Presbyterian Church about three miles northeast of Cape May City. A Presbyterian congregation which met at Coxehall was undoubtedly the nucleus of the Presbytery constituted in 1714. The church and locality was named after an icy cold spring near by. First church was a small log building erected in 1718. On July 2, 1723, the first Court in the County, of which records are preserved, was held in this church. The present structure dates from 1823.

The surrounding graveyard is the most interesting in the County. The oldest grave stone is that of Sarah Spicer, 1742, mother of Jacob Spicer, whose wealth, real estate speculations, and political activities are disclosed by an interesting extant diary. Joseph Whillden, died 1748, son of the pioneer of that name and a great grandson of John Howland, the Pilgrim of Plymouth, and his wife, Mary Whillden, 1743, are the next oldest graves.

The most famous ministers of this church were Reverend Daniel Lawrence (died 1766, and buried here), the Reverend Moses Williamson and Reverend Dr. Samuel Finley, who afterward became President of Princeton University.

At Cold Spring was erected, in 1699, the earliest water mill in the County. It was owned by John Carman.

SCHELLINGER'S LANDING. On Sewell's Inlet at the northern edge of Cape May City. During the Revolutionary War a base for armed pilot boats and privateers, fitted out in part by Cape May citizens, for protection of shipping entering the Bay.

CAPE MAY CITY. Formerly known as Cape Island. The earliest bathing resort along the Atlantic Coast. Mentioned as such by John Bringhurst in a letter dated 1765 and by numerous advertisements in Philadelphia papers. After boat and rail connections were established with Philadelphia, Baltimore and Washington, it was the resort of the early Presidents of the United States and members of Congress. The early hotels at which they stopped have been replaced by modern structures. The name Congress Hall is reminiscent of Cape May's having been frequently the summer White House and congressional summer playground.

CAPE MAY POINT. Called Stites Beach until 1876 when the name was changed to Seagrove. Boston, New York and Philadelphia newspapers, between 1712-1748, refer to the landing and depredations of various Spanish and French privateers at and near Cape May Point. Captain Kidd known to have landed here several times. Old tree known as Kidd's Tree stood near the light-house until about 1893. One of Kidd's landings here is mentioned in a report of the Lords of Trade to the Lords Justices under date of August 10, 1669.

LILLY LAKE. Cape May Point. During the Revolution to prevent use of its fresh water by the British for the supply of their ships, the patriots dug trenches connecting this lake with the Ocean, making it salt. Later the trenches were filled in and in time the water again became fresh.

SITE OF COXEHALL. About four miles north of the Point of the Bay Shore Road. Seat of the first proprietary or manorial system of land holding. Built about 1690. The cellar of the old house is still to be seen and it is planned to mark this inter-esting site. The earliest meetings of Presbyterians and Baptists appear to have been held here.

Vicinity of NEW ENGLAND TOWN, or TOWN BANK, or CAPE MAY TOWN, or PORTSMOUTH, or FALMOUTH (above referred to). Built on a bluff overlooking Bay about a quarter of a mile north of Coxehall. The first permanent inhabitants of the County came from Cape Cod and Long Island and settled and conducted their whaling, fishing, and fur industries here. The earliest known burial ground in the County was here. The settlement began before 1685 and continued for about thirty-five years. Due to the encroachment of the sea, the last traces of the first settlement were washed away by about 1750. (The Society of Colonial Wars in the State of New Jersey plans to place an appropriate marker at the nearest adjacent point on the Bay Shore Road).

FISHING CREEK or NORBURY LANDING. Site about 1735 of second oldest mill in the County, a fulling mill for manufac-ture of homespun cloth. It was owned by Captain Richard Downs.

CUMBERLAND COUNTY

Cumberland County is bounded on the south and south-west by Delaware Bay, northwest by Salem County, north-east by Gloucester and Atlantic Counties and southeast by Cape May County. Cumberland County was organized in 1747, having been prior to that time a part of Salem County. It was named by Governor Belcher in honor of the Duke of Cumberland.

BRIDGETON. The first person known to have settled where Bridgeton now stands was Richard Hancock, who after he ceased to be Surveyor-General for John Fenwick, came to the site of Bridgeton and built a saw mill on Indian Fields Run, now called Mill Creek. This mill, built shortly before 1686, stood just below the present bridge at the foot of Pine Street. Traces of the dam still remain.

The bridge over the Cohansey was built, resting on cribs sunk in the water, as early as 1716, it being referred to in a survey of that date. The place was called Cohansey Bridge until 1765 when in the Minutes of the Court, it is called Bridgetown. The Court was moved from Greenwich to Cohansey Bridge February, 1748, and it became the County Seat. Upon the establishment of what is now the Cumberland National Bank, in 1816, the first President, General James Giles, had the name of the town, printed "Bridgeton," on its notes and this soon became the adopted name.

The people of Bridgeton were firm adherents of the cause of the Colonies in the Revolution, a company of soldiers being raised there, of which General Joseph Bloomfield was Captain and General Ebenezer Elmer, Lieutenant. This company served in the army of General Schuyler. Dr. Jonathan Elmer, a resident of Bridgeton was a member of the Revolutionary Congress and subsequently one of the first Senators under the United States Constitution. In 1779-80 the Patriots constructed a Letter of Marque schooner named Governor Livingston which made at least one successful voyage.

Places of interest:

1. First Presbyterian Church, organized 1792. The land upon which it stands was given in 1791 by Mark Miller in consideration of a promise made by his father Ebenezer Miller, a Friend. The building commenced in 1792, was finished in 1795, part of the money having been raised by a lottery. There are many noted men buried in the church yard.

   Dr. Jonathan Elmer, 1745-1817, Revolutionary Soldier and Senator.

   Dr. Samuel Moore Shute, 1762-1816, Revolutionary Soldier and member of Society of Cincinnati.

GENERAL EBENEZER ELMER, 1752-1843.
JUDGE LUCIUS Q. C. ELMER, 1793-1883.
COLONEL DAVID POTTER, 1744-1805.
DR. BENJAMIN CHAMPNEYS, 1774-1814.
MAJOR ALMARIN BROOKS, 1756-1824, member of Cincinnati.
CAPTAIN CHARLES CLUNN, 1749-1807.
GENERAL JAMES GILES, 1759-1825.
DAVID SEELEY, 1751-1802.
JOSHUA REEVES, 1757-1838.

2. Methodist Episcopal Church. Organized 1804. First church erected 1807. Present one built 1833. In this yard there are several soldiers:

CAPTAIN ABRAHAM WOODRUFF, 1773-1861.
FREDERICK FAUVER, 1743-1853, War of the Revolution.
JAMES FAUVER, 1793-1861, War of 1812.

3. Site of the home of Senator Jonathan Elmer, erected 1774. Torn down in 1926. 102 Broad Street.

4. Home of Colonel David Potter of the American Revolution. Built 1780. No. 65 Broad Street.

5. General James Giles Mansion. Built 1792. 143 Broad Street.

6. Robert Elmer House. Built 1815. No. 230 E. Commerce Street.

7. Jonathan Elmer House. Built 1807. No. 297 E. Commerce Street.

8. Ivy Hall. No. 31 West Commerce Street. Built in 1825 by David Sheppard. Long a school for girls.

9. Site of the old Parvin Tavern. Southeast corner of Commerce and Atlantic Streets. Built in 1725. Removed in 1825. Here was born Clarence Parvin, a tea burner at Greenwich.

10. Site of the home of Governor Elias P. Seeley, No. 101 E. Commerce Street.

11. Site of the home of Governor Joseph Bloomfield. No. 3 Franklin Street.

12. Home of General Ebenezer Elmer. No. 56 Vine Street.
13. Bridgeton High School. Corner of Broad and Lawrence Streets. Part of this building was the old West Jersey Academy, a private boarding school for boys. In the tower of the high school hangs "Bridgeton's Liberty Bell," which rang in celebration of the signing of the Declaration, 14 West Jersey Academy.

DEERFIELD. Settled about 1732 by a number of Presbyterian families who organized a religious society, building a log church about 1737. In this church the Rev. Gilbert Tennent, the Rev. Brainerd, the brother of the celebrated Missionary and others, officiated. The present church was built in 1771.

Points of interest:
1. Near Deerfield is the old Seeley House which was built about 1780 by Josiah Seeley. This is a fine type of colonial architecture and has recently been listed by the White Pine Association.

FAIRTON. This is the center of an early settlement made prior to 1690 by pioneers from Fairfield, Connecticut and so called Fairfield, later becoming Fairton. The township is still known as Fairfield. A church was established at Fairton not later than 1690. It was called the "Cohansey Church of Fairfield" and was independent until 1708 when it united with the Presbytery of Philadelphia. The first building was of logs, located at a place called New England Town Cross-roads. This spot is marked by a monument on the south bank of the Cohansey River, just below Fairton, where many ancient tombstones also mark the site. About 1717 the log church was replaced by a frame one in the southeast corner of the graveyard. This served until 1780, when the "Old Stone Church," now in its turn deserted, about a quarter of a mile down the road, was ready for use. The "Old Stone Church" served until 1837 when the congregation divided, one part building a brick church in Cedarville and the other part a handsome edifice in Fairton.

The Fairton church is the legal successor of the old Cohansey Presbyterian Church.

DIVIDING CREEK. Sixteen miles from Bridgeton. Site of a Baptist Church organized about 1749.

CEDARVILLE. Eight miles southeast of Bridgeton. Presbyterian Church organized by emigrants from Fairfield, Connecticut. One of its early ministers was the Reverend Mr. Exile.

GREENWICH. The town of Greenwich was settled by emigrants from New England and Ireland. Fairs were established at Cohansey (name usually given to this part of the country at that time) in 1694 and held in April and October of each year. County Court was first held at Cohansey, May, 1748. Greenwich was the scene of the New Jersey tea burning November 22, 1774. The Brig Greyhound sent by East India Company to Cohansey discharged its cargo at Greenwich. On Thursday, November 22, 1774, forty men disguised as Indians removed the chests from the cellar where they were stored, piled them in an adjoining field and burned them. Among those engaged in the tea burning were Dr. Ebenezer Elmer, Richard Howell, later Governor of New Jersey, the Rev. Andrew Hunter, James Ewing, father of a subsequent Chief Justice of New Jersey and others. The parties were sued to recover damages and were defended by General Joseph Bloomfield, Elias Boudinot, Jonathan Dickinson Sergeant and George Read, of New Castle, Delaware. The war having broken out, the suits were dropped. A considerable number of the tea burners are buried in the church yard of the old Presbyterian Church.

Points of interest:

1. Monument in the Market Square commemorating the tea burning.
2. The old Tavern. Built 1730.
3. The old Gibbon House built 1730.
4. Site of old Episcopal Church.

ROADSTOWN. Four miles from Bridgeton.

Points of interest:

1. Old Baptist Church founded about 1737.

2. Howell Homestead. Home of Richard Howell, later Governor of New Jersey, and of Lewis Howell. Situated on the road between Shiloh and Roadstown. Meeting place of the men of Bridgeton and Fairton before joining the tea burners. One of the daughters of the Howell household was the grandmother of Jefferson Davis, President of the Confederacy.

MILLVILLE. Eleven miles east of Bridgeton. Founded about 1796.

SHILOH. On the road from Cohansey. Founded in 1705 by Robert Ayres, a Seventh Day Baptist, who purchased two thousand acres of land, which he sold to the people of his own faith. The town was first known as Cohansey Corners. When the people tried to move the log church built there, it stuck at a point where six roads radiated from one place, whereupon Ayres announced that the "Ark of the Lord rested at Shiloh," and the name of the place was changed to Shiloh.

ESSEX COUNTY

Essex County was formed in 1675. The boundaries were first determined in 1709-10 and as then established included what is today known as Union County.

The land constituting Essex County was purchased from the Indians by the settlers of the City of Newark for fifty double hands of powder, 100 bars of lead, 20 axes, 20 coats, 10 guns, 20 pistols, 10 kettles, 10 swords, 4 blankets, 4 barrels of beer, 10 pairs of breeches, 50 knives, 20 horses, 850 fathoms of wampum, 6 anchors of liquor, and 3 troopers' coats.

BELLEVILLE. On the Passaic River, three miles north of Newark. Founded prior to 1682 and once known as Second River. Scene of battle September 27, 1778.

BLOOMFIELD. Three and one-half miles from Newark. During the Revolution, Bloomfield was the scene of acts of violence and plunder on the part of the Tories. The Presbyterian Church in Bloomfield was erected in 1796. Corner of Bloomfield and Liberty Streets. Memorial tablet to General Joseph Bloomfield dedicated November 10, 1923, gift of Major Joseph Bloomfield Chapter, D. A. R.

CALDWELL. The town of Caldwell is notable as birthplace of Grover Cleveland, twice President.

NEWARK. Settled May, 1666 by settlers from Guilford, Branford, and Milford, Connecticut. Named Newark in honor of the Reverend Abraham Pierson, Pastor of the settlers who came from Newark, England.

Barbour and Howe state the purchase price of the original township of Newark as 130 pounds New England currency, 12 Indian blankets, and 12 Indian guns.

By agreement no one could become a Freeman or Burgess of Branford (the name originally selected for Newark) except such as were members of some Congregational Church. In the first distribution of land, six acres were given to each settler as a homestead. In planning the town, the Upper Green, now Washington Square, was reserved as a market place, the Lower Green for a military parade ground, now Military Park.

The people of Newark May 18, 1775, agreed not to export to Quebec, Nova Scotia, etc., or to furnish provisions to the King's ships or boats. In the Winter of 1778, a detachment of the second battalion of the Continental Army was stationed at Newark. An engagement took place here January 25, 1778.

The first church erected in Newark, that of the Rev. Mr. Pierson, built in 1668, on a lot opposite to the present Presbyterian Church.

The first Presbyterian Church had, as its pastor about 1736, the Rev. Aaron Burr, father of Aaron Burr, Vice President of the United States, born at Newark September 24, 1757.

The Protestant Episcopal Church in Newark originated in 1734, being organized by some Episcopalians and dissatisfied Presbyterians, one of whom Colonel Josiah Ogden had been disciplined for saving his grain on a Sabbath in a wet harvest season. As a result of this organization, Trinity Church was established. The present church, standing in Military Park, is built on the site of the original church and retains the original tower.

The College of New Jersey, now Princeton University, was located in Newark from 1747 to 1756, Rev. Aaron Burr being President from 1748 to 1757.

Notable places:

1. Broad and Market Streets. Residence of William S. Pennington, Major in Revolutionary Army, Justice of Supreme Court of New Jersey 1804, Governor 1813-15, Judge United States District Court 1815-1826. His son, William Pennington, became Governor 1837-1843.

2. Broad Street, East side. Residence of Elisha Boudinot, Associate Justice of the Supreme Court of New Jersey, first depositor in the Newark Banking & Insurance Company, and one of the Associates of the New Jersey Company organized to found Jersey City.

3. Residence of Dr. Uzal Johnson, originally a surgeon in Colonial Service, who became a loyalist but escaped capture.

4. East side of Broad Street. Residence of Judge William Burnett.

5. The Parsonage, formerly stood at Broad and William Streets. Residence of Rev. Aaron Burr and his wife, daughter of the Rev. Jonathan Edwards. Birthplace of

RECTORY OF HOUSE OF PRAYER, NEWARK
Here Rev. Hannibal Goodwin Invented Photographic Films

LYONS FARM SCHOOL HOUSE
First School Erected in Newark

Aaron Burr, Vice President of the United States. Occupied by Rev. Alexander M'Whorter during the Revolution and for many years thereafter pastor of the Church.

6. Residence of Peter J. VanBeckel, Minister from Holland to United States.

7. Opposite the Parsonage, near southeast corner Broad and Fair Streets, later known as David Alling house, Frenchmen's Place, home of Talleyrand for six months 1794-5

8. Decatur House. Home of John Decatur, brother of Commodore Stephen Decatur who came to Newark to take part in the fox hunts and hunt balls at the Gifford Tavern, northeast corner Broad and Market Streets.

9. Petersborough on the bank of the Passaic River—erected 1735. Home of Colonel Peter Schuyler, an officer in the French and Indian War.

10. Cockloft Hall, near Petersborough. Erected 1750 by Nicholas Gouverneur. Tradition says that it is described in the Salmagundi Papers by Washington Irving and some have even claimed that the papers were written there.

11. Bronze tablet marking camp ground of Revolutionary soldiers erected here by Nova Caesarea Chapter, D. A. R., at Philip's Park, Elwood Avenue, Newark.

ORANGE. Three and one-half miles northwest of Newark. Founded about 1720.

Points of interest.

1. Old First Church, corner of Main and Day Streets.

2. Revolutionary Burial Ground with monument of dispatch rider by Elwell.

3. Home of Thomas A. Edison.

4. Eagle Rock.

MONTCLAIR. Old Crane Homestead, Washington's Headquarters October 26, 27, 1780. Marked by tablet erected by Eagle Rock Chapter, D. A. R.

GLOUCESTER COUNTY

Gloucester County, which originally included Camden and Atlantic Counties, is bounded on the northeast by Camden County; on the southeast by Atlantic County; on the south-west by Cumberland and Salem Counties and on the northwest by the Delaware River.

Gloucester County was created 1686 and included the territory lying between Pensauken and Oldman's Creeks. It was organized May 26, 1686, at Axwamus, now Gloucester. The courts sat alternately "at Axwamus and Red Bank." In 1837 Atlantic County took a large part of Gloucester County, and in 1844 Camden County was formed out of another portion of Gloucester County.

Points of interest are:

1. On the Camden-Woodbury Turnpike, passing through Westville, one will reach Princeton Avenue—Taking Princeton Avenue at Colonial Manor, one will reach Candor Hall or Ladd's Castle, said to be the oldest house of brick in Gloucester County. Built by John Ladd, Sr. who purchased the property in 1688. Ladd was engaged by William Penn to help lay out Philadelphia, which he accomplished to Penn's satisfaction. Now known as the Shivers Farm House.

2. Red Bank Battle Field, at right angles to trolley line on Hessian Avenue or Hessian Run Road from Colonial Manor on the Delaware River, the most historic spot in Gloucester County. Fort Mercer constructed here by Council of Safety and named after General Mercer who died at Princeton January 3, 1777. Battle field, is marked by two monuments, one erected to the gallantry of Lieutenant Colonel Christopher Greene who, with four hundred men, conquered two thousand Hessian troops in the British service at Red Bank October 22, 1777. A second

monument unveiled June 21, 1906, commemorated the battle of Red Bank. Count Donop, Hessian Commander, mortally wounded at the battle, was carried to Whitall Mansion and subsequently removed to the farm house of Joseph Low across Woodbury Creek where he died.

By Act of Congress twenty acres of land at Red Bank, including the fort, monuments, and site of the old mansion, are now a public park under care of the Gloucester County Board of Freeholders.

3. Site of the mansion. Home of Ann Whitall who on the day of the battle was spinning in her home. A cannon ball entered the house, falling in the room where she was spinning. She removed her wheel to the cellar and continued her work.

4. Fort Nassau. Cornelius Jacobsen Mey, the explorer, in 1625 entered the Delaware Bay and explored the Bay and River. He landed and built a fort at Sussacon on Big Timber Creek, which he called Fort Nassau. This was the first European settlement on the Delaware River. (See monument in Gloucester to commemorate Fort Nassau which cannot be precisely located).

WOODBURY. Settled in 1684 by John Wood of Lancashire, England, for whom the town was named. Woodbury was occupied briefly in the winter of 1777 by Lord Cornwallis with an army of British troops and subsequently by the New Jersey Militia.

Points of interest:

1. Friends Meeting House built 1717, with addition erected 1783. Used during Revolution as a place for care of wounded soldiers. Diary of Job Whitall records finding the house filled with sick soldiers, eleventh month seven, one thousand seven hundred and seventy-seven.

2. Friends Burial Ground. Graves of James and Ann Cooper Whitall who occupied Whitall Mansion during the battle.

Also John Cooper, member of Continental Congress in 1776.

3. 90 South Broad Street. Headquarters of Gloucester County Historical Society, once owned by John Lawrence, brother of Captain James Lawrence of "Don't give up the ship" fame, who resided with him and attended the Academy School in Woodbury.

4. 130 South Broad Street. Residence of Dr. Duncan Campbell, built and occupied by John Cooper, member of the Continental Congress, the Committee on Correspondence and Council of Safety. He was also Judge of the County Court. The house was used by Lord Cornwallis as headquarters during the three days he was in Woodbury.

5. Opposite to 130 South Broad Street, bronze Soldiers' Memorial to commemorate the dead of Gloucester County who fell in the World War. Designed by R. Tait McKenzie.

6. Laboratory of Colonel G. G. Greene, where is shown a cannon dredged from the Delaware River bearing Coat of Arms of George III from the British ship "Augusta".

NORTH WOODBURY. On Main Street—The graveyard and site of Presbyterian Church acquired August 10, 1721. Many Revolutionary Soldiers are buried in this graveyard. The log church on this site was used as a hospital by the Continental troops following the Battle of Red Bank.

CLARKSBORO. Three and one-half miles from Woodbury. Residence of Nathan P. Hoffman, in Colonial days, "Death of the Fox Inn," rendezvous of Gloucester Fox Hunting Club.

MICKLETON. On the farther side of Mickleton, the residence of Colonel Boddo Otto of Revolutionary fame.

SWEDESBORO, on Raccoon Creek, was settled by the Swedes about 1642. The British, during the Revolution, burned the school-house.

On Salem Road, Swedesboro, just after entering town, Trinity Episcopal Church, built by the Swedes on land purchased in 1703, consecrated June 17, 1705, rebuilt about 1786. The Swedish naturalist, Kalm, spent one winter at Swedesboro where he preached in this Church. Nicholas Collin, last of the pastors sent over by King of Sweden, was pastor here during Revolution. Subsequently he became pastor of Old Swedes' Church, Philadelphia. The Right Reverend John Croes, first Episcopal Bishop of New Jersey, preached here one hundred and twenty-five years ago, then being rector.

In the Cemetery of Trinity Church are buried Colonel Boddo Otto, Colonel Thomas Heston, Colonel Robert Brown, Captain John Daniels, and others of Revolutionary fame.

Passing through Swedesboro to Battentown or South Swedesboro, one comes to the house of John Hatton, Local Stamp officer of Salem and Revenue Collector of West Jersey under George III, who became a fugitive, joining the royal army. His property was confiscated in 1778.

Stratton Mansion, built in 1784, by Dr. Stratton, birthplace of Charles C. Stratton, member of Congress and sixteenth Governor of New Jersey. House now owned by descendants of James Gibbs. The Stratton house is back from the main road where the Old Kings' Highway used to run.

Porch's Mill, three miles below Swedesboro, on the Kings' Highway to Sharptown. Site of Moravian Church, built of brick, dedicated 1786, replacing log church dedicated August 31, 1749. Gloucester County Historical Society placed a tablet on Church August 31, 1907. A skirmish occurred with the British near the Church June 12, 1778.

On the road from Hendrickson's Mill to Bridgeport, half way between Bridgeport and Swedesboro, is Adams Meeting House, formerly known as Old Stone Church or Oak Grove Church, built 1793. Said to be oldest Methodist Episcopal Church in New Jersey.

On the Delaware River just off the road from Paulsboro to Thoroughfare, about one-quarter mile from Paradise Station, is the home of Tench Francis, one of the founders of the University of Pennsylvania and an associate of Benjamin Franklin. Cannon were placed in his farm yard during a fight with the British ships.

GLASSBORO. Ten miles southeast of Woodbury. Settled during the Revolution by Stanger & Company, composed of seven brothers from Germany, who established a glass factory. They had been originally at Wistar's Glass House in Salem County. The first successful manufactory of its kind in North America. It is said that the First City Troop of Philadelphia was formed in the house of the late Isaac Moffott.

BILLINGSPORT. On the Delaware River. Some say it was named after Edward Byllynge, purchaser of Lord Berkley's moiety of the Province. Site of a Revolutionary Fort constructed for the purpose of preventing the British fleet from communicating with Philadelphia. Billingsport was acquired by the Thirteen United Colonies July 5, 1776, destroyed by the British September 30, 1777. Cornwallis landed and made second attack on Red Bank November 18, 1777. Billingsport was occupied by New Jersey Militia during the War of 1812.

On March 15, 1778, Colonel Mawhood landed at Billingsport and marched up Salem Creek to Mantua Bridge and on the 16th fought the militia who retreated to Tomkins Farm where they halted and fought until forced to retreat to the vicinity of Colonel Boddo Otto's residence near Mickleton.

MANTUA. Just beyond Mantua on Mantua Creek is the Hendrickson Oak, the largest in New Jersey. Until a few years ago the Tatem Oak, near by on the same stream, was reputed to be the largest and oldest oak in America. It was conservatively estimated to be over eight hundred years old at the time of its accidental destruction by fire.

HUDSON COUNTY

This County, organized from the southern portion of Bergen County in 1840, is the smallest county in the State.

BERGEN. "Village of Bergen" founded 1616 by Dutch Colonists. Perhaps named from Bergen in Norway. Land purchased from the Indians 1658-9 by Director General Stuy-vesant and Council of the New Netherlands. After the Col-ony passed into the possession of the English, a charter granted by Governor Carteret to the town and freeholders of Bergen provided for a church and free school supported by a tract of land exempt of tax.

During the Revolution the Americans built a fort near the center of the village on land belonging to one Newkirk, while the British built a fort about a mile southeast of Van Vorts Hill. The battle of Bergen took place July 19, 1780.

Stephen Ball was murdered at Bergen Point by Tory Refugees September 15, 1781. At the close of the Revolution, Cornelius Hetfield, leader of the refugees fled to Nova Scotia. In 1807, on returning to Jersey, he was arrested for the murder of Ball, but discharged on habeas corpus by Judge Pennington, who held that he was within the protection of the Treaty of Peace of 1783.

The Dutch Church at Bergen, organized in 1660, is the oldest in the State. In 1680 the church was replaced by one of stone, octagonal in shape. In 1773 this church was removed and a new one was erected. In 1664 the first public school in the State was established with Engelbert Stenbuysen, the church clerk as master.

Points of interest:

1. The Sip Manor. Erected 1666 by Claas Ariance Sip, owned by his male descendants in 1902. Lord Cornwallis and his staff spent a night here in 1776 and tradition says

hanged three spies on a willow tree in the garden before leaving next day.

2. Appletree House. Academy Street off Bergen Square. Home of Herman Wagenen who owned it when Washington and Lafayette dined under the great appletree in the orchard, which was still standing when Lafayette visited Bergen in 1824.

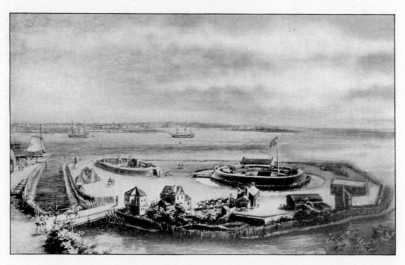

SCENE OF BATTLE OF PAULUS HOOK
Now Grand and Greene Streets, Jersey City

JERSEY CITY. In 1630, the patroonship of Pavonia was created in Michiel Parew of Amsterdam, embracing Hoboken. He did little to comply with the terms of his grant and the company bought him out. In 1633 the Company built two trading posts, one at Communipaw and one at Ahasimus or Jersey City. A third was built at Paulus Hook, named after Michael Paulusen, the patroon.

Points of interest:

1. Grand and Greene Streets. The battle of Paulus Hook took place here August 19, 1779. The British fort, then

STATUE OF PETER STUYVESANT, JERSEY CITY
Marking the Site of the Village of Bergen, the First Permanent Settlement in New Jersey

on an island, now in the heart of the City, was at or near Grand and Greene Streets. Stormed by "Light Horse Harry" Lee and three hundred men, including Allen McLane's dismounted dragoons, with a loss of two killed and three wounded.

2. Prospect Hall. End of Essex Street. Home of Col. Richard Varick, for thirty years President of Society of the Cincinnati. Erected 1807 by Major Hunt, mentioned by Washington Irving in Salmagundi. Varick, one of Washington's Secretaries and Mayor of New York while it was the national capitol. Lafayette entertained here in 1824.

3. The White House. Site at northwest corner Sussex and Hudson Streets. Owned by Colonel Varick, rented to a Mrs. Hedden, who here entertained Aaron Burr while he wrote or arranged his memoirs in 1830.

4. Van Vorst House. Wayne Street. Home of Cornelius Van Vorst. Sold by him to Edge family. Kitchen step was stone base of the statue of George III, Bowling Green, New York, which was overturned and melted in 1776. The stone which prior to becoming step to Van Vorst kitchen, was used to mark grave of Major John Smith of Royal Highland Regiment is now in New York Historical Society.

5. Prior House. Site of Prior House. Wayne Street. Quarter of a mile from Van Vorst House. House and mill of Jacob Prior used by General Mercer, General Greene, and Lord Stirling. Stopping point of Lee returning from Paulus Hook.

HOBOKEN. From Hobocan-hackingh "the place of the tobacco pipe." In 1643 a farm house and brew house were built north of Hoboken by Aert Van Putten, but town did not grow. In 1783 John Stevens purchased site of Hoboken for eighteen thousand three hundred and sixty pounds and put it on sale in town lots in 1804.

Points of interest:

1. Castle Point. Home of Colonel John Stevens. Part of the confiscated Bayard Estate. House built about 1784. Stevens workshop in Hoboken where he experimented and built the Phoenix Steamboat was on or near the site of Stevens Institute.

2. Astor Villa. Corner of Washington and Second Streets. Home in 1828 of John Jacob Astor. Fitz-Greene Halleck, the poet, Martin Van Buren, and Washington Irving often visited Astor here.

WEEHAWKEN. Probably from Awiehawken, name of a stream.

BUST OF ALEXANDER HAMILTON
Marking Scene of His Duel with Aaron Burr, Weehawken

Places of interest:

1. Highwood. Site of home of James Gore King lying between Bulls Ferry Road and River near Stevens Estate. Two of the King family descended from Rufus King, were

men of note—Chas. King, President of Columbia College and James Gore King, a banker known as "The Almighty of Wall Street." Here were entertained many people of note e.g., Daniel Webster, Nicholas Biddle, Charles Dickens and wife.

2. Dueling ground on King Estate where July 11, 1804 Alexander Hamilton was killed by Burr on the spot where his son, Philip Hamilton, had been killed. DeWitt Clinton, Commodore Perry, and others fought here.

GREENVILLE or Pamrapaugh. Three miles south of Jersey City.

RETIREMENT HALL, GREENVILLE

Retirement Hall. Built 1760 by Captain Thomas Brown, one of the chief slave dealers in the Colonies. Brown adhered to the Colonies. In September, 1781, during a storm, Prince William Henry, later William IV, took refuge at Retirement Hall. Passed out of hands of Brown's heirs and became finally home of Greenville Yacht Club.

HUNTERDON COUNTY

Organized in 1713. Originally part of Burlington County, named from Governor Robert Hunter. It included within its limits the present counties of Warren, Sussex, Morris, and Mercer.

LAMBERTVILLE or Coryell's Ferry. Founded by Manuel Coryell 1732. In 1797 called Georgetown and later named Lambertville from John Lambert, the first Postmaster.

Washington's Army, retreating before Howe and Cornwallis, crossed the Delaware at Coryell's Ferry, but Cornwallis was unable to cross because of the lack of boats. Washington stopped at the house of Richard Holcomb, General Greene at the home of George Coryell.

RINGOES. Settled in 1720 by John Ringo, who built where paths through the woods crossed, and there entertained travelers. Ringo's old tavern stood for seventy years. In 1778, scene of the repulse of the British sent from Trenton to destroy Flemington. When the party reached Pennington, a scouting

McKONKEY'S FERRY HOUSE, WASHINGTON CROSSING

party was sent out which was attacked at Ringoes. Geary, the Commander, was killed, and the rest of the party fled to New Brunswick, upon which the British retreated.

MERCER COUNTY

Mercer County, organized in 1838, was formed out of portions of Hunterdon, Burlington, and Middlesex Counties, and was named in honor of General Mercer, slain at the battle of Princeton.

WASHINGTON'S CROSSING, at one time called McKonkey's Ferry, later Bernardsville, or Eight Mile Ferry, on the Delaware where Washington crossed Christmas night 1776 previous to the attack upon the Hessians at Trenton. The site is being developed as a memorial park by the State. Tavern at Washington's Crossing figures in the crossing of the Delaware by Continentals.

COLUMBIA. Home of "Honest John Hart" one of the signers of the Declaration of Independence.

TRENTON. First settlement at the Falls of the Delaware made about 1679. Meeting house built about 1690 at Fallsington. Trenton, originally called Stacy's Mills after Mahlon Stacy, builder of the mills, was named from Colonel William Trent, who purchased a farm of eight hundred acres on Assunpink Creek in 1714. Trent was, in 1723, Speaker of the New Jersey Assembly and Commissioner for Hunterdon County. The County Courts which had been previously held at Hopewell were removed to Trenton in 1719. Battle of Trenton took place December 26, 1776.

Points of interest:

1. Five Points, where Washington's troops came into position and planted cannon, marked by Trenton Battle Monument.

2. Site of Hessian Sentry Post, opposite St. Mary's Cathedral.

NEW JERSEY BANK OF THE DELAWARE, NOW WASHINGTON'S CROSSING

Here Washington's Army Landed Christmas Night, 1776

3. House where Colonel Rahl died. Marked by a tablet. West side of Warren Street.

4. Home of Stacy Potts.

5. Site of Hessian Surrender, approximately near the Public Service Building, East State Street. Tablet marks spot.

6. Old Barracks, built by British at the time of French and Indian War, containing collection of relics and antiques of exceptional value. Building reproduced as New Jersey State Building at Sesqui-Centennial.

7. Douglas House, now facing on Stacy Park and not in original location. Washington held a council of war here January 2, 1777, with his officers, in which the plan of escape from Trenton and attack on Princeton was made. Original site of Douglas House marked by a tablet.

8. Governor's Mansion. South Warren Street. Site of the Hunterdon County Court House and meetings of Continental Congress.

9. Stone marking achievements of John Fitch, who sailed his steamboat on the Delaware prior to Fulton's boat on the Hudson.

10. Site of Triumphal Arch in honor of Washington, on South Broad Street.

11. Bloomsbury Court. South Warren Street. Home of William Trent, founder of Trenton. Later home of Cox family. Washington, Lafayette, and Rochambeau entertained here. An ash tree planted by William Trent still stands in the Colonial Garden.

12. The Hermitage. On the River Road. Erected by the Rutherfurd family prior to Revolution. Purchased by General Philemon Dickinson in July 1776 after the Declaration of Independence. John Adams was entertained

OLD BARRACKS AT TRENTON, ERECTED 1758-59
Home of Society of Colonial Wars in the State of New Jersey

here by General Dickinson in 1777 and later was here during the cholera scare in Philadelphia in 1798.

13. Bow Hill. Threequarters of a mile from Trenton. Lalor Road near Deklyn Lane. Red brick house famous as the home of Annette Savage of Philadelphia for whom the house was rented by Joseph Bonaparte. The house was jocosely called "Beau Hill."

14. Methodist Episcopal Church. South Broad Street.

15. Presbyterian Church. East State Street. Chartered by George II in 1756.

16. Friends Meeting House built 1739. Hanover and Montgomery Streets.

17. St. Michael's Episcopal Church.

ASSUNPINK CREEK. Site of Battle of Assunpink or Trenton Bridge January 2, 1777. Behind this stream watch fires were kept burning while Washington's Army marched from Trenton to Princeton. After taking Trenton December 26, the Continentals crossed the Delaware and remained for several days, returning again and taking possession of Trenton where they remained until January 2, 1777. The British Army on the opposite side of Assunpink, expected an engagement the following day. During the night Washington, leaving his fires burning and sentries posted, marched around the British Army toward Princeton, which he reached the following morning. The first information of his retreat received by the British was the sound of firing from the direction of Princeton.

LAWRENCEVILLE, originally called Maidenhead, about five and onehalf miles northeast of Trenton on the road between Trenton and Princeton. Site of a Presbyterian Church built 1752 and of Lawrenceville School. The British passed through Lawrenceville in pursuit of the Continental Army on the night of the Battle of Princeton.

PRINCETON. Site of Princeton University, formerly The College of New Jersey. The College, originally chartered by

STONEY BROOK BRIDGE, PRINCETON

John Hamilton, acting Governor 1746-7, was first located at Elizabeth, where Rev. Jonathan Dickinson was President. Subsequently it removed to Newark where Rev. Aaron Burr became President. In 1757 it removed to Princeton where Nassau Hall, first college building, was erected and named at the request of Governor Belcher in memory of King William III. Nassau Hall was occupied by the British as a barracks and stable during the occupancy of the town. The original building was partially destroyed by fire in 1802 but the stone walls remaining standing were utilized in its re-erection. The chapel had a picture of George II which was shot from the frame during the battle and later replaced by a picture of Washington by Peale.

Points of interest:

1. Princeton Battle Monument.
2. Clarke House.
3. Morven.
4. Nassau Hall.

NASSAU HALL, PRINCETON

CONGRESS HALL, PRINCETON

5. Monument to General Mercer.

6. Princeton Cemetery.

7. Quaker Meeting House.

8. Stoney Brook Burial Ground.

9. Tablet marking road to Morristown.

10. Monument to British and American Soldiers.

11. Tusculum. Home of John Witherspoon—in the suburbs of Princeton.

12. Constitution Hill.

13. Battlefield Farm.

14. Castle Howard.

15. Beatty House.

16. First Presbyterian Church.

17. Prospect. Farm house of Colonel George Morgan.

Princeton was the birthplace of Richard Stockton, a signer of the Declaration of Independence, who is buried in the Friends Burial Ground near Princeton. Commodore William Bainbridge, Rev. John Witherspoon, a signer of the Declaration of Independence and President of Princeton College are buried in the Princeton Burial Ground, as is also Aaron Burr, once Vice President of the United States.

MIDDLESEX COUNTY

By an Act of March, 1682, the Province of East Jersey was divided into the four Counties of Bergen, Essex, Middlesex and Monmouth. Middlesex County then comprised much more territory than now, as part was set off to Somerset County in 1688, 1850, and 1858; part was set off to form Mercer County in 1838, part added to Monmouth County in 1844 and part to Union County in 1858. As at present constituted, it is bounded on the north by Union County; on the east by Staten Island Sound and Raritan Bay; on the southeast by

Monmouth County; on the southwest by Mercer County and on the west by Somerset County.

PERTH AMBOY or "Perth Town." On the Raritan Bay at the junction of Raritan River and Sound. Was named in honor of the Earl of Perth, who was one of the Associators. It was located at Ambo Point and the name Perth Amboy is a combination of Perth and Ambo. The town site is supposed to have been selected by Governor Carteret and the first charter was granted August 1718 during the administration of Gover′ nor Robert Hunter. Early Provincial Governors resided here— Governor Lawrie, Andrew Hamilton, Lord Neill Campbell, Robert Hunter, Jonathan Belcher, Francis Bernard, Thomas Boone, Josiah Hardy, and William Franklin.

Perth Amboy was, during Colonial days the site of bar′ racks built in 1758 and 1759, occupied by troops returning from the siege of Havana. The place is industrial and large terra cotta works are here located.

BUILDING OF THE PROPRIETORS OF EAST JERSEY, PERTH AMBOY
and Residence of William Franklin, Last Royal Governor (Now Westminster Hotel)

Principal points of interest:

1. The Court House Market, formerly the office of the Secretary of the Province, now in possession of St. Peter's Church.

2. Residence of Governor William Franklin. Built in 1764, now known as Westminster Hotel, where Franklin came in 1775 to urge, but without success, his son, William Franklin, to join the American cause.

3. Kearney Cottage. Built 1780, where Elizabeth Lawrence Kearney, or Madame Scribblerus, taught her half-brother, Captain James Lawrence the love of poetry. Kearney Cottage now owned by the Perth Amboy Historical Society, has been moved from its former location.

4. Bartow House. Moved from its original location and remodeled. Original site now occupied by the Baptist Church. Here William Dunlap, theatrical manager, art historian, and critic did his first drawings.

5. Parker Castle built in part a century before the Revolution. Here many notable personages gathered. It is still standing in its original location. Used by English as a barracks and a hospital in the Revolution.

6. St. Peter's Church established in 1685. Used as a stable during the Revolution. A stone from the original church is inserted in the rear wall of the present church.

7. Foundation and part of the first story of the present City Hall are of the original building built about two hundred years ago.

8. East Jersey Proprietor's Building, about seventy-five years old containing records of more than two hundred and fifty years ago, the earliest times of the Province.

9. East Jersey Club. Its present home on High Street was one of the first buildings built in the city. It was a former

residence of Neill Campbell, one of the prominent immi-grants from Scotland.

10. The Presbyterian burial ground on State Street dates back to the early part of the 18th century.

NEW BRUNSWICK, or Prigmore's Swamp. On west bank of Raritan River, twenty-six miles northeast of Trenton. Set-tled by John Inian and Cornelius Longfield 1681, originally named Inian's Ferry. Named New Brunswick in honor of British Royal house. Royal charter granted in 1730. First inhabitants were from Long Island, many of them Dutch.

Rutgers College was the eighth college founded in Ameri-can Colonies. Charter granted in 1766 by William Franklin, Governor. Formerly called Queen's College. Charter revised in 1770. In 1825 name was changed to Rutgers in honor of Henry Rutgers, a Colonel in the Continental Army.

Points of interest:

1. Bell Tavern. Stopping place of Franklin, Adams and Rut-ledge, Commissioners to meet Lord Howe at Staten Island Conference. The Bell has been an Inn since 1729, first known as the Indian Queen, then the Bell, and recently modernized and renamed The Parkway.

2. Buccleuch. In Buccleuch Park. Occupied by the British at the time of the British occupation of New Brunswick. George Washington subsequently a guest of honor at Buccleuch. Home of Colonel Anthony Walton White, friend of Washington.

3. Whitehall Tavern. Dated 1756.

4. Neilson House, Burnet Street. Headquarters of Lord Howe, winter of 1776-1777.

5. Vale Mansion, dated 1760. Livingston Avenue and Car-roll Place. Built by Henry Gest. During Revolution the

place of refuge of Tom Payne when he fled to avoid arrest on charge of treason. The house bears the marks of cannon shot.

6. Dutch Church. Organized 1717.

7. Presbyterian Church 1739-40.

8. Episcopal Church built 1743. Bishop Seabury at one time Rector.

9. Home of William Paterson, Governor of New Jersey, member of the Constitutional Convention, United States Senator and Justice of the Supreme Court of the United States.

WOODBRIDGE. Woodbridge Township named in honor of the Rev. John Woodbridge, who, with a number of associates and their families, came from Newbury, Massachusetts, in 1665, and settled in Woodbridge, at the solicitation of Captain Philip Carteret, Governor of the Province of New Jersey. Chartered June 1, 1669.

The General Assembly of the Province met in Wood-bridge October 5, 1676, lasting four days, when it was decided that the Governor's salary should be paid in "peas, wheat or tobacco." Among the laws passed was one providing that "rowdies be put in the stocks for two hours for swearing, quarrelling, drinking liquor or singing vain songs or tunes on the Sabbath."

The Township Court established in 1669, was held in a building on the site where Mrs. F. G. Tisdall's residence now stands on Rahway Avenue.

In 1680, Rev. John Allen of England, was selected as pastor of the Town Church, built in 1675 on the "Kirk Green" near the spot now occupied by the Presbyterian Church.

The Presbyterian Church dates back to year 1669. The Presbyterian Burial Ground has burials prior to 1700. Here may be found the graves of Captain Daniel Britton, who died in 1733, General Nathaniel Herd, Captain Nathaniel Fitz Randolph, Captain David Edgar, Lieutenant James Paten, Colonel Samuel Crow, Colonel Benjamin Brown, General Clarkson Edgar, and a host of others.

Trinity Episcopal Church founded in 1711, was chartered by George III, December 6, 1769. The Episcopal Burying Ground dates from 1714.

The Quaker Burial Ground (now the Methodist Burial Ground) dates from 1707.

In 1751, James Parker, an apprentice of William Bradford, printer in New York, established a printing press. In 1761, Parker printed on his Woodbridge press the second volume of Nevill's Laws of New Jersey.

General Washington visited Woodbridge April 22, 1789, and stopped at the Cross and Key Tavern while on his way to New York to be inaugurated President.

Woodbridge was the scene of much fighting by the British, Tories, and Continentals during the Revolution.

Sewaren, now part of Woodbridge, has Governor Carteret's quarters to which the soldiers would come from Totenville to confer with the Governor.

CRANBURY. Settled about 1697 by Joseph Prickett. One of the oldest places in the State. In its vicinity David Brainerd, missionary to the Indians, labored.

Points of interest:

1. First Presbyterian Church, founded over two hundred years ago. The graveyard has many headstones dating back to the eighteenth century, and contains the remains of many soldiers of the Revolution.

2. Northwest corner of Main Street and Plainsboro Road. House occupied by General Washington prior to Battle of

Monmouth. Place of refuge of Aaron Burr after his duel with Hamilton.

3. John Wetherill House. King George's Highway between Cranbury and Dayton. Here lived John Wetherill, member of the New Jersey Colonial Assemblies and Provincial Congress, and a Colonel in the Revolution.

4. John Wicoff House. West of Cranbury on Plainsboro Road. Here lived John Wicoff, a Revolutionary soldier who fought in Washington's Army at Battles of Trenton, Princeton, and Monmouth.

MONMOUTH COUNTY

Monmouth County, created by Act of Assembly held at Elizabethtown March 7, 1683, and named by Colonel Lewis Morris after the place of his nativity, Monmouthshire, Wales, was first settled by English from Gravesend, Long Island. In 1685 the Dunnottar Castle prisoners, imprisoned by Charles II for opposition to Established Church, sailed in the Caledonia with George Scot, Laird of Pitlochie, September 5, 1685. They stranded on the Jersey Coast December, 1685. Many of them settled near the Old Scot's (now Tennent) Church. They were followed a few years later by Dutch from Long Island and about 1700 a number of French Huguenots settled in the county. The boundaries of the county first roughly defined in 1675 and definitely settled in 1714, remained as established in 1714 until 1850, when Ocean County was established from it.

FREEHOLD or Monmouth Court House, about 30 miles from Trenton. County Courts held here 1735. Scene of Battle of Monmouth June 28, 1778, between Clinton's Army retreating from Philadelphia and the Continental Army under Washington in pursuit.

Freehold and vicinity settled mainly by Scotch. The town originally called Topanemus, had its origin in the building of a Court House in 1715 when it became the County Seat.

Notable places:

1. Monmouth Battle Monument. Corner Stone laid June 28, 1878. Unveiled November 13, 1884.

2. Marker at Molly Pitcher's well, near road from Freehold to Englishtown near Pennsylvania Railroad. Molly Pitcher died in Carlisle, Pennsylvania, January 22, 1832, and is buried in the English Graveyard.

3. Marker on Englishtown Road showing where Washington met Lee.

4. Hankinson Mansion on "Old Burlington Path," or Main Street. Headquarters of Sir Henry Clinton, June 27, 1778. House erected 1755.

5. Old Tennent, formerly Old Scots, Church built 1751. Three miles southeast of Englishtown and three miles from Freehold. Originally called Old Scots Church, then Freehold Church. In memory of John Tennent and William Tennent, Jr., it took the name of Tennent Church. It was the successor of an older church built 1730, which seems to have been the successor of the Old Scots Meeting House built 1692 by the original Scotch settlers on or near the site of the Old Scots Burying Ground. The outlines of the old church can still be seen on the road leading to Englishtown about two miles from Freehold, in Marlboro Township. The oldest grave in the yard is that of Rev. John Boyd, first Minister of the Church, who died August 30, 1708; the oldest in the present Tennent Church Yard is that of Alice Smith, died 1739. Rev. Wm. Tennent, Pastor of the Church for over forty-three years, who died March 8, 1777, is buried under the floor of the central aisle. At one corner is buried Lieutenant Colonel Monckton of the British Army, killed June 28, 1778.

6. St. Peter's Church. Throckmorton Street. opposite Pennsylvania Railroad Station. St. Peter's Church had its

HEADQUARTERS OF SIR HENRY CLINTON, FREEHOLD, JUNE 27, 1778

OLD TENNENT CHURCH, NEAR FREEHOLD

origin in a Quaker Meeting House built by George Keith, about a mile west of Marlboro, about 1695 and never finished. On Keith's defection from the Quakers about 1702, the building was taken over by the Church of England and was used by that church in 1751. It was removed to its present location in Freehold between that time and 1763, the new church being built in part with the timbers of the old church. A piece of land was donated at Freehold in 1709 for the erection of a church. The church, which was not completed for three-quarters of a century, was consecrated May 8, 1836, by Bishop Doane. The oldest tombstone in the old Topanemus or Freehold graveyard is that of Elizabeth Clark, died December 25, 1697.

7. Cincinnati Hall. First house in Freehold burned by the British on the day of the Battle of Monmouth. Re-erected shortly after the Revolution by Dr. Thomas Henderson on the old foundations. Named Cincinnati Hall in honor of the Society of the Cincinnati.

8. First Court House constructed 1715 of wood—destroyed by fire December 17, 1727. The second Court House built 1730, and used for more than seventy-five years, was standing in June, 1778. The third Court House erected 1806 was destroyed in 1873. Original site marked in 1905 by stone from Rocky Hill placed by Samuel C. Cowart, bearing bronze tablet with inscription "Site of the Old Monmouth County Court House used as a hospital in the Battle of Monmouth, June 28, 1778."

9. Pew in old Tennent Church endowed by Tennent Chapter, D. A. R., June 14, 1921, in memory of George Washington.

ADELPHIA, formerly Blue Ball. About three and one-half miles south of the Court House in Freehold. At a short distance north of the hamlet is Shumar's or Morgan's Mill. There Colonel Daniel Morgan with his corps of riflemen waited during the whole of the day of June 28, 1778, for orders to take part in the Battle of Monmouth. The Bethesda Methodist Church at Blue Ball, founded about 1780, is the oldest Metho- dist Church in the State. Present church built in 1849.

MARLBORO on road from Freehold to Bradevelt. The Old Brick Church—known as the Reformed Church of Navasink and afterwards as the Dutch Reformed Church dates to days of the earliest Dutch settlements; was organized about 1699. Present building erected 1826.

ENGLISHTOWN. Birthplace of General David Forman, Commander of the Jersey Troops at Germantown, friend of Washington, Judge of the County Court, and Member of the Council of the State. Village House erected in 1732. It was here orders were framed for the court martial of General Charles Lee.

MIDDLETOWN. Sixteen miles northeast of Freehold. Mid- dletown, a settlement made by men from Gravesend, Long Island, in 1665, was originally a Baptist settlement. The church, organized about 1668, was the first Baptist Church in the State. The first building was torn down in 1734, and another constructed, which was succeeded by the present church in 1832.

On the Main Street, nearly opposite the Baptist Church, is an old burying ground known as the Presbyterian Yard, the oldest grave being that of John Boune, died 1715.

FRENEAU—once called Mt. Pleasant.

Point of interest:

Mount Pleasant Hall, about one and one-half miles out from Middletown on the Middletown Turnpike, built 1752 by the father of Philip Freneau, the Poet of the Revolution. Fre- quently visited by James Madison in his young days. Nothing but remains of the house are to be seen now. Freneau and his wife are said to be buried in the family burying ground at Mt. Pleasant.

MATAWAN. Burrows Mansion still standing in the village, erected in the first half of the eighteenth century. Tradition says, the first New Jersey company formed for the Revolutionary War was mustered in the garden, marching to Long Island to join the army of Washington.

GRAVELLY POINT. One mile north of Beacon Hill. Spot where British embarked for New York after the Battle of Monmouth, also scene of the murder of Captain Joshua Huddy.

SANDY HOOK. First lighthouse built 1762. Seized and fortified by British. Attacked by Monmouth County Militia under General Forman.

COLT'S NECK. Five miles from Freehold, on a neck of land formed by two branches of Swimming River. Home of Joshua Huddy, whose house at Colt's Neck was attacked in 1780 by a party of Loyalists commanded by one Tye, a mulatto. Huddy, who was captured at the defense of Tom's River, March 1782, was carried to New York and executed April 12, 1782, by the Loyalists. He was buried at Freehold with the honors of war. For this "barbarous outrage against humanity" the Board of Loyalists was forbidden to remove any further prisoners and was abolished by Sir Guy Carleton.

SHREWSBURY. Settled by emigrants from Connecticut 1664. Episcopal Church established about 1702, chartered June 3, 1738. Friends Meeting House, established prior to 1672, visited by George Fox, George Heath, and others. Original Meeting House now in possession of the Hicksite Branch of the Society, the Orthodox Friends having built a new Meeting House at the time of the separation.

Presbyterian Church founded about 1735. Chartered 1749 in connection with Freehold and Allentown.

MORRIS COUNTY

Morris County, taken from Hunterdon County by Act of Colonial Assembly of 1738-9, included within its limits territory now forming Sussex and Warren Counties. It was named after Lewis Morris, Governor of the Province.

MADISON, settled by emigrants from Long Island. In Colonial days known as South Hanover, subsequently as Bottle Hill and in 1834 named Madison by vote of the people. In 1780, when the British tried to surprise Washington at Morris-town, they reached Bottle Hill, but snow, rain, and hail made the road impassable, and they were compelled to retreat.

Points of interest:

1. Sayre House. Ridgedale Avenue, built in 1745 by Daniel Sayre. Opened to Continental officers and soldiers during Revolution. Used by General Anthony Wayne as headquarters while the army was in camp at Loantaka Valley.

SAYRE HOUSE, MADISON

2. Bottle Hill Tavern, 127 Main Street. Building originally stood at Main Street and Waverly Place. Removed to present location 1923. Owned and occupied by Madison Historical Society.

3. Presbyterian Church organized about 1752.

4. House of Major Miller.

5. Tomb of Major Miller.

WHIPPANY. Four miles north of Morristown. Site of first Presbyterian Church in Morris County erected about 1718. First military company in Morris County was formed in the vicinity of Whippany in the Fall of 1775, under the command of Captain Morris.

CHATHAM. About three and one-half miles east of Madison.

Points of interest:

1. Ward House, dated 1740.

2. Talmadge Homestead, where Washington was a guest.

3. Shepard Kollock's printing house where New Jersey Journal was published. Opposite Morrell House.

4. Morrell House. East Main Street. Opposite Presbyterian Church where Washington frequently stopped.

5. Day Mansion. Elmwood Avenue. Site of present Ogden Memorial Church.

6. Hamblin House. Northeast corner of Main Street and Elmwood Avenue. Home of Mrs. Hamblin, where General Lafayette was entertained in 1825.

7. Bonnell Homestead. Watchung Avenue. Home of Mrs. Bonnell, who baked bread all night to provide soldiers sleeping on her floors with food for their march to Yorktown, Virginia.

8. Chatham Bridge over Passaic River. During the winter of 1779-80, New York Bay froze to such an extent that the

British Cavalry could cross to New Jersey. Chatham Bridge was guarded day and night to prevent the British reaching Morristown, Washington's Headquarters. The bridge was also the scene for the exchange of Prisoners.

MORRISTOWN. About fifty miles from Trenton, twenty-six miles from New York. Settled between 1700 and 1720.

First Presbyterian Church erected in 1740. The Court House in 1755. Scene of the encampment of Washington's Army, (1) in January 1777, after the Battles of Trenton and Princeton, (2) in 1779-80. In 1777 General Washington was quartered in Freeman's Tavern. In 1779-80 his quarters were at the residence of Colonel Jacob Ford, now owned and pre-served by the Washington Association of New Jersey, which contains a fine collection of relics. Open to public free of charge daily, except Thanksgiving, Christmas and Sundays. The town is the birthplace of General Daniel Morgan.

Points of interest:

1. Dickerson Tavern. Spring and Water Streets. Scene of Court Martial of Benedict Arnold, presided over by General Robert Howe.

2. Campfield House. 5 Olyphant Place. Scene of courtship of Elizabeth or Betsy Schuyler by Alexander Hamilton, 1779-80, occupied at time by John Cochrane, Surgeon General of the Continental Army. The house is now owned by the Morristown Chapter, D. A. R. Open to public free of charge Tuesdays and Fridays throughout the year.

3. Tempe Wick's House. Jockey Hollow Road. Frame house occupied by Wick family. Made notable by exploit of Tempe Wick who hid her horse in her bedroom for three days.

4. Liddell House. Jockey Hollow Road. Built of stones used in the fireplaces of the soldiers' huts in the Revolution.

TEMPE WICK'S HOUSE, MORRISTOWN

5. Fort Nonsense. On western outskirts of the town is a high hill known as Fort Nonsense. Site of series of earth-works built by order of General Washington to protect encampment from possible assault. Because the earth-works were never used, the hill received the name. Site of earth-works marked by boulder erected by Washington Association of New Jersey.

6. Sun-dial erected by Morristown Chapter, D. A. R., on the grounds of Memorial Hospital, where in 1777, at an open air service of the Presbyterian Church, General Washington partook of Holy Communion.

7. Monument on Jockey Hollow Road erected by Morristown Chapter, D. A. R., in memory of Captain Adam Bettin, Tenth Pennsylvania Regiment, shot in the mutiny of his troops, January 1, 1781.

8. Stone boulder placed on the Morristown Green by Morristown Chapter, D. A. R., to mark the site of the County Court House and jail standing in the Revolution.

WASHINGTON'S HEADQUARTERS, MORRISTOWN

9. Stone erected by Morristown Chapter, D. A. R., on grounds of the Presbyterian Church to mark site of original First Church where General Washington worshipped while living in Morristown.

10. Speedwell. Home of Samuel Morse and Alfred Vail, where the first successful experiment in electric telegraph was made in 1838.

11. Monument in the burying ground of the Old Presbyterian Church erected by Morristown Chapter, D. A. R., in memory of Revolutionary soldiers buried there.

12. Camp of Stark's Brigade, Kemble Mountain. Stark's Brigade encamped on the southeastern slope of Mt. Kemble. A monument built of stone has been raised on the side of the mountain from stones included in the chimneys of the Revolutionary Soldiers' huts.

13. Burnan Park. Site of fortification and signal station.

14. Hoyt's Corner. Tablet to Peter Kemble.

GREEN VILLAGE. Tablet erected by Morristown Chapter, D. A. R., near center of village marking route of Washington and his army to Morristown after Battle of Princeton.

MT. VERNON. Tablet erected by Morristown Chapter, D. A. R., showing route of Washington and his army to Morristown after Battle of Princeton.

MENDHAM. Founded in 1713. Six and one-half miles southwest of Morristown. Site of mutiny of Pennsylvania Line, January, 1781.

Points of interest:

1. Hill Top Church, left side of Main Street, built about one hundred years ago on the site of the original church erected 1745, which was used as a military hospital in the winter of 1777.

2. Black Horse Tavern, built 1745 by Ebenezer Byron.

3. Drake House is situated about one mile from the village on the road to Morristown. Headquarters of Colonel Robinson and Chevalier Massillon in the winter of 1779-80.

LOANTAKA VALLEY CAMP GROUNDS. Loantaka Valley, now called Spring Valley, one and one-half miles southeast of Morristown. Site of Washington's encampment after the Battle of Princeton, Washington being quartered in Arnold Tavern, his first headquarters at Morristown.

HIBERNIA. Furnaces at Hibernia and Mount Hope, under the proprietorship of Charles Hoff, Jr., and John Faesch, supplied shovels, axes, refined iron ore, cannon balls, grape shot, etc., for use of the Continental Army. The employees were exempted from enlistment. Ruins of the Iron Works still to be seen.

HANOVER. Site of parsonage of Rev. Jacob Green, Pastor of the first church erected at Hanover. His home was here from 1746 to 1790. Elected to the Provincial Congress, which adopted the Revolutionary Constitution. An early opponent of slavery. Parsonage is still standing near the Hanover Postoffice.

TROY HILLS. Beaverwyck, home of Lucas Von Beaverhoudt. Noted for its hospitable entertainment of soldiers, both British and American during the Revolution. Practically a neutral ground. Tradition says that Major André first saw Washington here. The house is now the home of Sarah Condit.

OCEAN COUNTY

Ocean County, organized about 1850 out of the southern portion of Monmouth County, is bounded on the north by Monmouth County, on the east by the Atlantic Ocean, on the south by Great Bay, and on the west by Burlington County.

TOMS RIVER. County Seat. On the banks of Toms River. In the Revolution a fort or block-house was erected a short distance north of the bridge on a hill east of the road to Free-hold. In 1782 the block-house was attacked by the Associated Loyalists. It was defended by Captain Joshua Huddy and a garrison until, the ammunition being expended, he was forced to surrender. The town was burned with two mills and the block-house, the cannon spiked and thrown into the river. Huddy was hanged by the Loyalists at Gravelly Point, the highlands of Navasink, April, 1782.

CEDAR CREEK BRIDGE. Scene of engagement December 27, 1782, between the Burlington County Light Horse, under Captain Shreve and John Bacon, with a band of Loyalists. The Loyalists escaped, owing to aid given by some of the inhabit-ants, who opened fire upon the militia. Bacon was subsequently killed in an engagement with Shreve's Light Horse at Egg Harbor.

PASSAIC COUNTY

Passaic County formed in 1837 out of northern part of Essex County and western part of Bergen County. Iron ore and sand-stone are found in the County.

PATERSON. Established 1791 by a society organized by Alexander Hamilton, named in honor of Governor, afterward Justice, Paterson. Fine views of surrounding country can be obtained from Garrett Rock and Preakness Mountain near Paterson.

PREAKNESS. Five miles from Paterson. Site of home of Colonel Theunis Dey, whose mansion was Washington's Head-quarters from July 1 to July 29, 1780.

POMPTON LAKES. Settled by Dutch in 1682. Site of old homesteads still occupied by Schuyler and Outwater families. Formerly noted for its iron furnaces. Ringwood Mine fur-

HOME OF COLONEL THEUNIS DEY, PREAKNESS
Washington's Headquarters, July 1 to 29, 1780

nished the iron melted into cannon balls and carried by ox teams to West Point. Pompton was the site of the mutiny in 1780-81 of the Jersey Line.

LITTLE FALLS. Quarry between Singac and Totown furnished stone for Trinity Church, New York City.

About two miles north of Little Falls at Lower Preakness on west side of highway is a two-and-a-half story stone mansion erected about 1740 by Colonel Theunis Dey, used by Washington as his headquarters in the summer and fall of 1780. Colonel Dey was commandant of Bergen County Regiment of New Jersey Militia, serving during the entire Revolution. He also represented Bergen County in New Jersey Assembly at different times between 1761 and 1783.

SINGAC in Little Falls Township. Site of gate for collection of tolls on old Newark and Pompton Turnpike. Settled by a Hollander, John Riker.

SALEM COUNTY

Salem County was a part of the land embraced in Fenwick's Colony which extended from Oldman's Creek to Cohansick or Cohansey Creek. It was originally settled by a company of English from New Haven, Connecticut, under the leadership of Theophilus Eaton. The settlement, made on the farm known as the Amos Harris Farm at the mouth of Salem Creek, did not last long. The next settlement was at Fort Elfsborg, which was built about March 1, 1642-43, on the eastern Bank of Salem River near its mouth. This fort, constructed by Swedes under Governor Printz, was commanded by Sven Skute. Subsequently it became untenable because of mosquitoes and was called Myggenborg, the "Mosquito Fort."

CARNEY'S POINT. A Dutch settlement antedating Fenwick. The Indian Deed to Fop. Janssen Outhout, dated 1664-5, is still on record.

FINN'S POINT or Pompion's Hook or Fort Mott. Settled early and first called Finn's Town Hook.

PEDRICKTOWN, named for Rodger Pedrick, whose one thousand acres was surveyed June 17, 1682.

PILESGROVE. Named for Thomas Pile, whose ten thousand acres was laid out to him in 1682.

PENN'S NECK. Thirty-two thousand acres set off to William Penn in 1706.

FENWICK GROVE. Upper Mannington, home of John Fenwick, who lived, died, and is buried there. Marked by monument erected July 4, 1924, on Highway from Salem to Woodstown.

WISTARBURG. Two miles east of Alloway. Site of the Glass Works of Casper Wistar, whose factory was built 1739.

FRIESBURG. Founded 1748 near Alloway by Germans who had worked in Wistar's Glass Works.

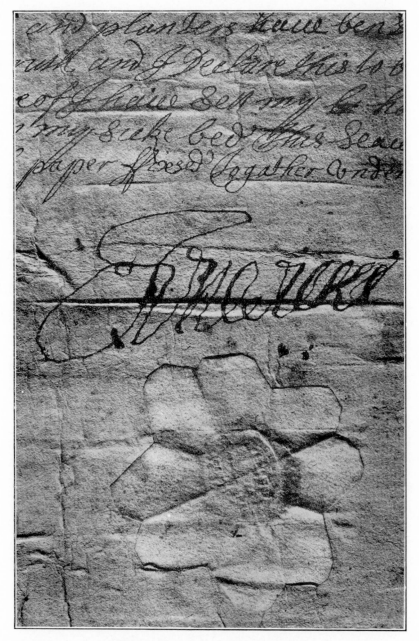

SIGNATURE AND SEAL OF JOHN FENWICK

German Lutheran Church started 1740.

PITTSGROVE or Champney Corner, commonly called Pole Tavern. Eastern boundary of Fenwick. The first regularly equipped military organization for defense with barracks organized there. The barracks are still standing. The volunteer company formed was officered by Captain Jacob duBois and Lieutenant Peter duBois, who, together with many privates of the same name, were descendants of Louis duBois, a Huguenot, who settled in New Paltz, New York, in 1660.

Points of interest:

1. Site of Champney's Tavern, commonly called Pole Tavern, because a Liberty Pole was erected on the green in front of the tavern during the Revolution.

2. The old barracks.

3. On the green in front of the town hall is a brass six pounder bearing the date 1763. Its history is as follows: Taken from the Italians by Napoleon Bonaparte in his second campaign in Italy, afterward captured from the French by the Duke of Wellington in the Spanish Peninsula campaign; later taken from the British at Lundy's Lane by General Scott; finally rendering service in the Mexican War and returning with Colonel Dickinson to his home in Salem County, New Jersey.

DARETOWN. Two miles below Pole Tavern. Here stands the ancient brick church built in 1740, called the Pittsgrove Presbyterian Church. It was built on land obtained from Louis duBois, who with his brother, Barent duBois, emigrated from New Paltz, New York, to Pittsgrove Township, purchased in 1714 by their father, Jacob duBois, son of Louis duBois, the Huguenot, from Daniel Cox of Burlington, New Jersey.

The graveyard contains the remains of many Revolutionary soldiers among them being those of Colonel William Shute.

He was a Lieutenant in the French and Indian War under General Samuel Hunt, New Jersey Provincial Troops, as well as a Colonel in the Revolution. He served at the battle of Quinton's Bridge, and was one of those listed as a target for British vengeance by Colonel Mawhood.

QUINTON'S BRIDGE. Alloways Creek, about three miles from Salem. Scene of desperate engagement between the British under Colonel Charles Mawhood and Continentals March 18, 1778. The Continental Militia defended Hancock and Quinton Bridges, seeking to prevent the British crossing. Site marked by small monument at Quinton erected by Oak Tree Chapter, D. A. R., on Main Street at the homestead of Captain William Smith, October 17, 1908.

HANCOCK HOUSE, HANCOCK'S BRIDGE

HANCOCK'S BRIDGE. Hancock House. Home of Judge William Hancock, owner of the house and friend of the Governor, who was shot in the attack of the British upon the house. The Continentals ultimately retired from Quinton's Bridge and the British took possession later returning to Philadelphia. The attack on the Hancock House is known as the "Massacre at Hancock Bridge." Tablet on Hancock Bridge House to commemorate massacre, erected by Oak Tree Chapter, D. A. R., 1903.

WOODSTOWN. Named from Jackanias Wood, whose home is still standing there. Settled early by the Friends. Meeting House erected about 1726.

"Niggers' Glory" built 1755. Noted for meals served at 15c and rum 11½c per quart.

Woodsboro House, built 1797.

RAMAPO. Two and one-half miles from Woodstown. Site of the Seven Stars, built 1765.

SALEM. On Salem River, thirty-four miles southeast of Philadelphia. The first English settlement in New Jersey was probably in the vicinity of the site of Salem. After the Duke of York had granted the Province of New Jersey to Berkeley and Carteret, Edward Byllynge purchased from Berkeley a tract for one thousand pounds. In 1675, Fenwick sailed from London in the Griffin, and landed at Fort Elfsborg September 23, 1675, and went to the spot named by him Salem. The town was laid out in 1675, incorporated in 1695. In 1774 the people collected $700.00 for the relief of the City of Boston. March 15, 1778, Colonel Mawhood landed at Billingsport and advanced to Salem which he occupied about March 16, 1778.

Points of interest:

1. Friends Meeting House, head of Walnut Street.

2. Alexander Grant House, erected 1721. Market Street, west side, home of Salem County Historical Society.

3. Capitol House, erected 1691. Foot of West Broadway.

4. Guilford Hall, erected 1687. Johnson Street near East Broadway.

ANCIENT OAK, SALEM

5. St. John's Episcopal Church. East side of Market Street, deed to congregation given 1721.

6. Salem Oak.

7. Court House marked by tablet erected by Society of Colonial Wars on 250th Anniversary of founding of Salem.

TABLET ON COURT HOUSE AT SALEM

SOMERSET COUNTY

Somerset County was first settled by the Dutch and was set off from Middlesex County as a separate County in 1688.

BASKING RIDGE. Settled by Scotch Proprietors.

Points of interest:

1. Log Church erected about 1700, replaced in 1749 by wooden structure destroyed in 1839.

2. Site of White's or Veal's Tavern where General Charles Lee was captured by the British December 13, 1776.

3. Old oak at Basking Ridge said to have been over two hundred years old.

BASKING RIDGE OAK

VICINITY of Basking Ridge. One mile southeast of Bask-ing Ridge stood "the Buildings," the house erected in 1761 by Lord Stirling, a Major General in the Continental Army dur-ing the Revolution and subsequently the scene of many social events. A part of the original house is incorporated in the present structure.

PLUCKEMIN. Six miles northwest of Somerville. Site of encampment of part of the American Army during the winter of 1778-9. The village was raided by the British in December, 1776. St. Paul's Church was used as a temporary prison for two hundred and thirty British soldiers taken prisoners, at Battle of Princeton.

[91]

In the village graveyard is buried Captain William Leslie, son of the Earl of Leven, killed January 3, 1777, at Princeton. His monument was erected by Dr. Benjamin Rush of Philadelphia.

VICINITY of Pluckemin.

1. McDowell House between Pluckemin and Lamington.

2. Site of McCrea homestead, located near McDowell home. Home of the Rev. James McCrea, father of Jane McCrea.

SOMERVILLE is of Revolutionary or post-Revolutionary origin. At the out-break of the Revolution, a tavern stood on the site of The Somerville House. Millstone was the County Seat and when the Court House there was burned by the British October, 1779, the County Seat was removed to Somerville, then called Raritan, about 1784. A Court House and jail built of logs was constructed. The place continued to be known as Raritan until 1809-10. The Church of Raritan was organized March, 1690. The church was burned in 1779 by the British under Colonel Simcoe, and was subsequently rebuilt in combination with the Court House, the congregation contributing one-half of the total cost, and the County paying the balance.

The first Somerset County Court House was erected at Six Mile Run, now Franklin Park. The site was marked November 15, 1910, by a boulder placed by the Historical Society of Somerset County, bearing a bronze tablet furnished by the Society of Colonial Wars in the State of New Jersey. It is placed upon the southeast corner of the lot facing the road from Franklin Park to New Brunswick.

Somerville was the home of Frederick Frelinghuysen, a member of the Continental Congress at the age of twenty-two, who saw service at Trenton and Monmouth, and subsequently became United States Senator.

WALLACE HOUSE, SOMERVILLE

1. Wallace House. Washington's Headquarters for six months during the winter and spring of 1778-9, now owned by Revolutionary Memorial Society of New Jersey and used as a museum.

2. Memorial fountain erected by Frelinghuysen Chapter, D. A. R.

3. House of Dirk Middaugh, west of Wallace House, built 1681.

4. Coejeman's House. Built 1737, said to have been occupied by Lafayette during Washington's stay at the Wallace House.

5. Site of old Fritt's Tavern. Was Hotel Somerset. Main Street, corner of Grove Street.

6. First Dutch Reformed Church of Raritan, north side of Main Street between Bridge and Grove Streets.

7. House of Rev. John Frelinghuysen built of Holland brick, 1751, by congregation of First Reformed Dutch Church

and known as "Old Dutch Parsonage and First Theo-logical Seminary." It has been removed several hundred feet from its original site.

8. Four boulders with bronze tablets marking sections of Washington's Line of March from Princeton to Morris-town, erected by Frelinghuysen Chapter, D. A. R., one at entrance to Somerville, at the corner of Warren Street and Court House Grounds, one at Allen's Tavern, one at entrance to Pluckemin on grounds of Kenilworth Inn, and one at Griggstown.

9. Site of home of Lord Neill Campbell, son of the Duke of Argyle, sometime Governor of New Jersey, located on Raritan River, three miles west of Somerville.

VICINITY. The Frelinghuysen Mansion is located on the south side of the road on the outskirts of Millstone.

Two miles southwest of Somerville on Old York Road, mansion once owned by Ferdinand Van der Veer, the old home of William Paterson, a Justice of the Supreme Court of New Jersey, Governor of New Jersey 1790, member of the Con-stitutional Convention of the United States and Justice of the Supreme Court of the United States, for whom the City of Paterson was named.

MILLSTONE. The second Somerset County Court House was at Millstone. On October 28, 1911, the Society of Colonial Wars in the State of New Jersey, the Sons of the Revolution and the Somerset County Historical Society erected a bronze tablet on the site to commemorate this building.

FINDERNE. In the town of Finderne, about three miles from the Wallace House, is the Van Veghten House, which was occupied by General Greene and his staff during the winter of 1778-9.

BOUND BROOK. Supposed to have been originally called Boundary Brook. Settled about 1700. Americans defeated at

Bound Brook 1777 by British, under Cornwallis. Site of engagement marked by boulder, at east end of Main Street, bearing bronze tablet commemorating the Battle of Bound Brook April 13, 1777, between General Lincoln and the British Troops.

SOUTH BOUND BROOK. Staats or Latourette House. Headquarters of Baron Steuben while Continental Army was at Camp Middlebrook.

On road from Bound Brook to Somerville, Van Horne House. West of the Middlebrook, north of the highway from Bound Brook to Somerville, home of Philip Van Horne, a Judge of the Common Pleas of Somerset County in pre-Revolutionary days. In winter of 1778-9, occupied by Lord Stirling as his headquarters.

CAMP MIDDLEBROOK. Site of the encampment of Washington and his army from May 28 to June 14, 1778. The first camp was in Washington's Valley about one mile from Martinsville, three miles from Bound Brook. Three earth forts were erected guarding the Valley, one of which still exists in a good state of preservation. The second encampment at Middlebrook was from November 28, 1778, to June 3, 1779. The site of the encampment has now been taken over by the Borough to be maintained as a public park.

ROCKY HILL. Fourteen miles from Somerville, four miles from Princeton, mansion built 1734 by Judge John Berrien, appointed Judge of Somerset County 1739 and Justice of the Supreme Court 1764. Washington's headquarters from August 24 to November 10, 1783. Here he wrote his farewell address to the Army. Rocky Hill has been furnished by different Societies and contains a collection of most interesting relics.

BERNARDSVILLE. Tablet marking route of Washington to Morristown.

RESIDENCE OF JUDGE JOHN BERRIEN AT ROCKY HILL
Where Washington Wrote His Farewell to the Army

SUSSEX COUNTY

Northwestern County of the State. It was organized June 8, 1753, from a portion of Morris County. During French and Indian Wars the settlements on the upper Delaware were subject to Indian incursions. In November, 1755, Colonel John Ruderson, with the Sussex Militia, sent to the Moravian Missionaries at Bethlehem for powder and was refused, but the powder was later furnished on threat to burn the town. When the Indians destroyed Gnadenhutten in Pennsylvania, the Sussex Militia went to assist the people of the back settlements and forts were built at Broadheads, Colverts Mills, and other places for defence of Sussex County. In May, 1756, the Indians appeared in Paulis Kill, Sussex County, and the Colony denounced the Lenni-Lenape as enemies, rebels, and traitors because of treaty violation. In the pre-Revolution days the Sussex delegates to Colonial Congress opposed the resolutions relative to Governor William Franklin July 16, 1774.

The freeholders of Sussex County met at Newton and adopted resolutions expressing allegiance to the Crown and urging the repeal of the Boston Port Bill and offering to become parties to redress the grievances of the Colonies. Early in the struggle, a Tory Association was organized in Sussex County, the members of which resolved not to pay the taxes levied by the Province or to attend militia musters. In August, 1776, it was reported to Congress that a search for lead mines in Sussex County had disclosed "Symptoms thereof" about four miles from Newton and flints "exceeding promising" near Beaver Run, Sussex County.

"The Farmers Journal and Newton Advertiser" was published in Sussex County 1796-98 by Elliot Hopkins and William Houston.

In Sussex, the slave population in 1790, was one forty-fifth. In 1820 the County was the most populous in the State. Zinc, lead and other minerals of commercial importance are found in the County.

NEWTON. County Seat. Sixty-eight miles from Trenton. Court House here authorized by Act of 1761.

Two miles south of Newton in region of Big and Little Muckshaw is Moody's Rock. Site of hiding place of Bonnell Moody, a noted Tory, and his followers. Tradition says that Moody was captured in the American Ranks near Morristown and hung as a spy.

ANDOVER WORKS. Six miles south of Newton on direct road to Newark. Steel mill and iron works or smelter built 1761, operated by the English, taken possession of by order of Continental Congress 1778, furnishing iron and steel to the Continental Army. Tradition says that the Hudson River chain was produced at Andover Forge.

HAMBURG. Six miles north of Franklin, 12 miles northeast of Newton.

Monument near Lawrence Homestead marking encamp-
ment of Washington's Army on March from Newburg to
Morristown. Monument erected by Marquise Ellen Kays Mc-
Laughlin, a member of the Chinkchewanska Chapter, D. A. R.

SWARTWOUT'S POND. Named from Swartwout, an officer
in British Colonial Service obnoxious to the Indians because of
his activities. Scene of Indian Massacre in which Swartwout
was slain.

OLD MINE ROAD. Constructed by the Dutch, who operated the mines about 1650. In Sussex County, at Port Jervis,
it passes through a brick house and the village of Minnisink,
parallel to the Delaware River. It begins at Kingston, New
York.

MINNISINK FORT

MINNISINK. Minnisink was the scene of Battle of Minnisink, July, 1781, with the Indians, commanded by Brant. West-
brook House or Fort. Oldest house in Sussex County. Family
living in Minnisink as early as 1701.

FLATBROOKVILLE. Van Campen Inn. Stopping place of John Adams, second President of the United States.

UNION COUNTY

Organized in 1857. Was formed out of Essex and Middlesex Counties. The English settled in the County in 1666 at Elizabeth. Eighteen battles or engagements took place in Union County in the Revolution. A list of dates and places follows:

Ash Swamp ....May, 1777
Ash Swamp ....June, 1779
Connecticut Farms ....June 7, 1780
Connecticut Farms ....June 23, 1780
Elizabethtown ....December 17, 1776
Elizabethtown ....January 25-30, 1780
Elizabethtown ....June 6, 1780
Elizabethtown Point ....July 21, 1778
Elizabethtown Point ....June 8, 1780
Rahway Creek ....September 30, 1777
Rahway Meadows ....June 26, 1781
Springfield ....December 17, 1776
Springfield ....February, 1777
Springfield ....October, 1779
Springfield ....June 23, 1780
Spanktown (Rahway) 1777
Westfield ....March 8, 1777
Westfield ....June, 1777

ELIZABETH. Four miles from Newark. The Borough of Elizabeth was incorporated February 8, 1739, and was the first English and second permanent settlement in the State. Philip Carteret, first Governor of East Jersey, landed at the Point which he named Elizabethtown in 1665, in honor of Lady Elizabeth Carteret, wife of Sir George Carteret.

The Colonial Assembly met here May 26-30, 1668, and continued so to meet until 1682. In 1686 it met at Amboy, and subsequently alternated between Amboy and Burlington.

December 1, 1774, Elizabethtown approved the recommendation of the Continental Congress regarding non-importation and non-exportation, and on February 13, 1775, resolved to break off trade, etc., with Staten Islanders as unfriendly "to the liberties of America." Elizabeth suffered greatly during the Revolution from Tory raids, and was the scene of four battles or engagements, viz: December, 1776, January 25-30, 1777, and June 6, 1780. Two other engagements took place at the Point July 21, 1778, and June 8, 1780.

Places of note:

1. Hetfield House. Foot of Pearl Street, near Elizabeth River, supposed to have been built 1667, conveyed to Matthias Heathfield December 5, 1673. Still owned by his descendants who spell the name Hetfield.

2. St. John's Parsonage. 633 Pearl Street. Built 1696 by Andrew Hampton. Purchased in 1749 by Trustees of St. John's Church.

3. Williamson House. Corner of Pearl and Williamson Streets. Built in 1776. Now used by St. Elizabeth's Hospital. Home of General Matthias Williamson, Revolutionary officer, who was the father of Governor Isaac H. Williamson and grandfather of Chancellor Benjamin Williamson.

4. The Old Chateau. 408 Rahway Avenue. Built 1760. Home of Cavalier Jouet, grandfather of Chancellor Williamson. Jouet was a descendant of Daniel Jouet of Angers, France, and Marie Cavalier, a sister of the "Camisard" Jean Cavalier, famous in the time of Louis XIV. Cavalier Jouet was a Tory and his property was confiscated.

5. DeHart House. 101 Rahway Avenue, corner of Cherry Street. Built 1766. Home of John DeHart, member of the Continental Congress and Mayor of Elizabeth.

6. Site of Red Lion Inn. Broad Street and Rahway Avenue. Now occupied by Public Library. Inn built about 1734. In 1764, called Marquis of Granby. In 1771 name changed to "Red Lion." General Washington on the way to his first inauguration stopped and held a reception at the Red Lion.

BOXWOOD HALL, ELIZABETH

7. Boudinot Mansion or Boxwood Hall, 1073 E. Jersey Street. Probably built about 1750. Home during Revolution of Elias Boudinot, who, as President of the Continental Congress, signed the treaty of peace with Great Britain. The body of Rev. James Caldwell, murdered by the British at Elizabethtown Point, was exposed to the view of the Revolutionary Army on the steps of this house and Boudinot made an address. Home owned subsequently by Jonathan Dayton, Speaker of the United States House

of Representatives and United States Senator, for whom Dayton, Ohio was named. Lafayette entertained here in 1824. Now "Home for Aged Women." Marked by bronze tablet placed by the Boudinot Chapter, D. A. R., 1899.

8. Carteret Arms. 16 S. Broad Street. Used as a tavern prior to 1728. Resort of British officers. Purchased in 1913 by the Elizabeth Historic and Civic Association, now occupied by the Woman's Club.

9. Graham's Tavern. Northeast corner Broad and Jersey Streets, also known as City Tavern. Noted for the prominent persons who patronized it, including Dr. Barnet, Lord Stirling, Judge Chetwood, Matthias Williamson, and others.

10. General Scott House. 1105 E. Jersey Street. Home of Dr. William Barnet, Revolutionary Surgeon, built 1763. Plundered by the British in 1781. Later owned by Colonel John Mayo of Richmond, Virginia, whose daughter became wife of Lieutenant General Winfield Scott.

11. St. John's Church. Broad Street. Organized by Rev. John Brooke, cornerstone laid June 24, 1706. Incorporated by Royal Charter 1762. Present church erected 1859. Font presented by Cavalier Jouet. Rev. Thos. Bradbury Chandler, Revolutionary rector, was a Loyalist and fled to England. Church used as a stable by British, who tried to burn it.

12. Nathaniel Bonnell House. 1045 E. Jersey Street. Built before 1682. Reputed to be the second oldest house in Elizabeth.

13. Minute Man erected Union Square, marking site of Continental Outpost at battle of June 8, 1780.

BELCHER MANSION, ELIZABETH

14. Governor Belcher Mansion. 1046 E. Jersey Street. On original lot of John Ogden, one of first settlers. Governor Belcher lived here from 1751 to 1757, entertaining many prominent persons including George Whitefield and Jonathan Edwards. House has been called "the cradle of Princeton University." Residence of William Peartree Smith, Revolutionary Patriot, later residence of Governor Aaron Ogden, who entertained Lafayette here in 1824. Marked in 1925 by bronze tablet placed by Daughters of the Founders and Patriots of America.

15. Site of Gracie House. 1123 Elizabeth Avenue. Bought in 1764 by Captain Isaac Lawrence from Jonathan Hampton and Elias Dayton, later owned by Jonathan Dayton and Elias Boudinot, who conveyed it to Dr. Abraham Clark, son of a signer of the Declaration of Independence.

16. Old Fort. Thompson's Avenue near Bridge Street. House built by Captain John Hunlake, bears date 1734.

17. First Presbyterian Church. Broad Street. Organized 1664. Burned 1780. Rebuilt 1784. The Revolutionary Pastor, Rev. James Caldwell, a strong patriot, was shot at Elizabethtown Point while under a flag of truce.

18. Site of Second Government House built 1680 by Governor Carteret. Across the alley, west of Penal's store at 1150 Elizabeth Avenue, half way between the Avenue and the Creek. Advertised in 1785 as "that large commodious famous brick house built***** by a former Governor of New Jersey for the seat of government. Situated on the river running through the town, on which is a very good wharf."

19. Liberty Hall. Morris Avenue. Built in 1772 by William Livingston, Revolutionary Governor of New Jersey. Scene of the marriage of Governor Livingston's daughter to John Jay, first Chief Justice of the United States Supreme Court. William Henry Harrison, ninth President of the United States, eloped from this house with a granddaughter of Livingston, the daughter of Susannah Livingston and John Cleves Symmes. House later owned by Lord Bolingbrook and Susan Livingston Kean, great grandmother of United States Senator Kean of New Jersey.

CONNECTICUT FARMS, now Union. Near Newark. Scene of battle June 7, 1780, between six thousand British, including Coldstream Guards and Germans, and Americans under General Maxwell, resulting in defeat and retreat of British. Home of Rev. James Caldwell, minister of the First Presbyterian Church of Elizabethtown. June 25, 1780, Mrs. Caldwell was shot at Connecticut Farms by a Tory. The town was destroyed November 24, 1781.

Tablet erected by State to Mrs. Caldwell.

RAHWAY or Spanktown. Supposed to have derived its first name from an Indian Chief named Radwack. The first dwellings were built about 1720.

CHURCH AT CONNECTICUT FARMS (NOW UNION)

Abraham Clark, one of the signers of the Declaration of Independence, was born about one and one-half miles from Rahway on the road to Elizabeth. Though not a lawyer, he was known as the "Poor man's Counselor." Died June 1794 and buried in Presbyterian Cemetery at Rahway.

SPRINGFIELD. On turnpike from Elizabeth to Morristown. Six miles from Morristown at the foot of Short Hills. Town founded about 1717 when the Briant family came to Spring-field from Hackensack.

Springfield was the site of a bitterly contested engagement between the Continentals and Militia under the command of Major Generals Green and Dickinson and the British, June 23, 1780. The British forced the passage to the streams protecting the town and burned it. During the battle "Parson" Caldwell took hymn books from the church and threw them to the soldiers for wadding, shouting "Put Watts into 'em, boys." Battle commemorated in Bret Harte's poem "Caldwell of Springfield," and by monument erected by Sons of American Revolution.

PLAINFIELD or Mill Town. Originally of Quaker origin. Quaker Meeting House built 1788 at Watchung and North Avenue, still standing.

Monument in Green Brook Park, Plainfield, commemorating camp at Blue Hills.

WASHINGTON'S ROCK near Plainfield. Point from which General Washington, in May and June 1777, watched New York Harbor to ascertain the direction in which the British Army, under Lord Howe, sailed. Marked by Continental Chapter, D. A. R., 1912. Site created a park by the Legislature, 1913.

Washington's Rock Park Lodge contains antique furniture given by the Continental Chapter, D. A. R.

WARREN COUNTY

Warren County, the first post-Revolutionary County, was organized in 1824 out of the southern portion of Sussex County, a County with rich farming lands and with abundant stone and iron.

HOPE. Moravian Settlement founded about 1769, abandoned about 1805.

Washington entertained at Hope July 26, 1782, while going from Bethlehem, Pennsylvania, to Newburg, New York. The idea of the founders of Hope was a new Bethlehem but it made no impression on the public and was abandoned.

OXFORD. Old furnace five miles from Belvidere, established about 1740. First Presbyterian Church founded 1744. Oxford was then known as Upper Greenwich.

HACKETTSTOWN. Visited by Washington in 1780 after Arnold's treason while on tour of inspection of Army.

BELVIDERE. Incorporated 1845, though settled many years prior. Sent troops to service in War of 1812.

WASHINGTON. Monument erected in memory of Peggy Warne and her services May 30, 1915 by Peggy Warne Chapter, D. A. R.

SUGGESTED TOURS

ROUTE 1. Trenton, Robinsville, Hightstown, Cranbury, Dayton, New Brunswick, Bound Brook, Somerville, Rocky Hill, Princeton, Lawrenceville, Trenton.
Total Mileage, 75.

ROUTE 2. Trenton, Hightstown, Freehold, Adelphia, Toms River, Mt. Holly, Burlington, Bordentown, Crosswicks, Trenton.
Total Mileage, 110.

ROUTE 3. Trenton, Washington's Crossing, Lambertville, Ringoes, Flemington, Whitehouse, Bedminster, Morristown, Madison, Chatham, Springfield, Elizabeth, Plainfield, Bound Brook, Somerville, Princeton, Lawrenceville, Trenton.
Total Mileage, 135.

ROUTE 4. Trenton, Bordentown, Burlington, Mt. Holly, Moorestown, Haddonfield, Woodbury, Swedesboro, Woodstown, Salem, Quinton, Shiloh, Bridgeton, Millville, Glassboro, Camden, Beverly, Burlington, Bordentown, Trenton.
Total Mileage, 180.

ROUTE 5. Camden, Woodbury, Swedesboro, Woodstown, Salem, Hancock Bridge, Roadstown, Greenwich Pier, Bridgeton, Fairton, Bridgeton, Millville, Glassboro, Mantua, Woodbury, Camden.
Total Mileage, 120.

ROUTE 6. Camden, Glassboro, Millville, Dennisville, Cold Spring, Cape May, Cape May Point, Cape May Court House, May's Landing, Egg Harbor, Green Bank, Batsto, Hammonton, Indian Mills, Medford, Haddonfield, Camden.
Total Mileage, 200.

ROUTE 7. Camden, Haddonfield, Berlin, Hammonton, Batsto, Green Bank, Tuckerton, Cedar Creek, Toms River, Lakehurst, Mt. Holly, Moorestown, Camden.
Total Mileage, 155.

ROUTE 8. Camden, Moorestown, Mt. Holly, Lakehurst, Toms River, Lakewood, Adelphia, Freehold, Colts Neck, Shrewsbury, Middletown, Perth Amboy, New Brunswick, Princeton, Lawrenceville, Trenton, Bordentown, Burlington, Beverly, Camden.
Total Mileage, 200.

ROUTE 9. Jersey City, Newark, Elizabeth, Rahway, Woodbridge, Perth Amboy, Middletown, Red Bank, Shrewsbury, Freehold, Tennent, Englishtown, Dayton, New Brunswick, Bound Brook, Plainfield, Elizabeth, Newark, Jersey City.
Total Mileage, 140.

ROUTE 10. Jersey City, Newark, Elizabeth, Plainfield, Bound Brook, New Brunswick, Princeton, Somerville, Pluckemin, Bedminster, Morristown, Madison, Chatham, Springfield, Elizabeth, Newark, Jersey City.
Total Mileage, 145.

ROUTE 11. Jersey City, Hoboken, Weehawken, Fort Lee, Englewood, Hackensack, Paterson, Pompton Lakes, Franklin Furnace, Newton (Swartswood Lake), Andover, Hackettstown,

Washington, Clinton, Somerville, Bound Brook, Plainfield, Elizabeth, Newark, Jersey City.
Total Mileage, 167.

ROUTE 12.　Jersey City, Newark, Elizabeth, Rahway, New Brunswick, Princeton, Lawrenceville, Trenton, Washington's Crossing, Lambertville, Ringoes, Flemington, Whitehouse, Bedminster, Morristown, Madison, Chatham, Springfield, Elizabeth, Newark, Jersey City.
Total Mileage, 150.

ROUTE 13.　Jersey City, Newark, Elizabeth, Rahway, New Brunswick, Princeton, Lawrenceville, Trenton, Bordentown, Crosswicks, Yardville, Hightstown, Freehold, Colt's Neck, Shrewsbury, Red Bank, Middletown, Perth Amboy, Woodbridge, Rahway, Elizabeth, Newark, Jersey City.
Total Mileage, 160.

STEUBEN HOUSE, NEW BRIDGE

BIBLIOGRAPHY

Smith's History of New Jersey.

History of Bergen County, N. J., 1630 to 1922.

Bottle Hill and Madison by William P. Hirst Tuttle.

Historical Collections of New Jersey, 1844, Barbour & Howe.

Historic Houses of New Jersey, W. J. Mills.

Old Roads from the Heart of New York, Sarah Comstock.

New Jersey Colony and State, Francis B. Lee.

Gordon's History and Gazetteer of New Jersey, 1834.

History of Burlington and Mercer Counties, Woodward and Hageman, 1883.

History of St. Mary's Church, Burlington, Hills.

The History of Burlington, New Jersey, Schemerhorn.

Sketches of Greenwich, New Jersey, Bessie Ayres Andrews.

Colonial and Old Houses of Greenwich, N. J., Bessie Ayres Andrews.

William Benedict's Book About New Brunswick.

History of Fenwicke Colony (Salem), Shourds.

History of Gloucester, Cumberland and Salem Counties, Chas. E. Shepard.

Chatham. Philhower's History of Chatham.

Story of an Old Farm, Melick.

Historic Princeton, Edwin Mark Norris.

Princeton, V. Lansing Collins.

Princeton and Its Institutions, Hagerman.

History of Elizabeth, J. C. Connolly.

History of Elizabeth, Hatfield.

Revolutionary History of Elizabeth, N. J.

Historic Sketches of Camden, Howard M. Cooper.

History of Camden, Powell.

History of Orange, New Jersey, David L. Pierson.

Bloomfield, Old and New, Joseph F. Folsom.

E. P. Tanner's Province of New Jersey, 1908.

History of the Colony of Nova Caesarea, or New Jersey, Samuel Smith.

Isadore Mulford's Civil and Political History of New Jersey.

W. A. Whitehead's East Jersey Under the Proprietary Governments.

Jersey Waggon Jaunts, Heston.

LIST OF ILLUSTRATIONS

Page

Trinity Church, Newark.....................................Frontispiece

The Hermitage, Hohokus.. 13

Old St. Mary's Church, Burlington.................................. 15

Revel House, Burlington... 17

Crosswicks Meeting House.. 21

Home of John Woolman, Mt. Holly................................. 23

Buttonwood Tree, Haddonfield..................................... 26

The Indian King Tavern, Haddonfield.............................. 27

Rectory of House of Prayer, Newark............................... 41

Lyons Farm School House.. 41

Scene of Battle of Paulus Hook................................... 49

Statue of Peter Stuyvesant, Jersey City............................. 50

Bust of Alexander Hamilton, Weehawken............................ 52

Retirement Hall, Greenville....................................... 53

McKonkey's Ferry House, Washington's Crossing...................... 54

Washington's Crossing 56

Old Barracks at Trenton... 58

Stoney Brook Bridge, Princeton.................................... 60

Nassau Hall, Princeton.. 61

Congress Hall, Princeton 62

Building of the Proprietors of East Jersey and Residence of William Franklin,
    Perth Amboy 64

Headquarters of Sir Henry Clinton, Freehold........................ 71

Old Tennent Church, near Freehold................................ 71

Sayre House, Madison 75

Tempe Wick's House, Morristown................................... 78

Washington's Headquarters, Morristown............................. 79

Home of Colonel Theunis Dey, Preakness............................ 83

Signature and Seal of John Fenwick................................ 85

Hancock House, Hancock's Bridge.................................. 87

Ancient Oak, Salem 89

Tablet on Court House at Salem.................................... 90

Basking Ridge Oak 91

Wallace House, Somerville 93

Residence of Judge John Berrien, Rocky Hill........................ 96

Minnisink Fort 98

Boxwood Hall, Elizabeth 101

Belcher Mansion, Elizabeth 103

Church at Connecticut Farms, now Union........................... 105

Steuben House, New Bridge.. 110

INDEX

	Page
Absecon Beach	10
Adams, John	57, 66, 99
Adelphia	72
Amboy	99
Andover Works	97
André, John	81
Andros, Sir Edmund	6
Arcola	12
Arnold, Benedict	77, 107
Assunpink Creek	59
Atlantic County	10
Audubon, John James	25
Aylesford, Kate	10
Bainbridge, William	63
Barton, Clara	19
Basking Ridge	90
Batsto	23
Belcher, Jonathan, Governor, 6, 33, 60, 103	
Belleville	39
Bergen	5, 48
Bergen County	11
Berkley, Lord John	4, 5, 88
Berlin	23
Bernardsville	95
Berrien, Judge John	95
Beverly	19
Billingsport	47, 88
Blommaert	4, 28
Bloomfield	39
Bonaparte, Joseph	19, 20, 59
Bordentown	19
Bottle Hill	75
Boudinot, Elias	16, 18, 101, 103
Boudinot, Elisha	40
Bound Brook	95
Brainerd, David	68
Brant	98
Bridgeton	33
Bulls Ferry	12
Burlington	5, 14, 99
Burlington County	14
Burnet, William	6
Burr, Aaron	40, 42, 51, 53, 63, 69
Byllynge, Edward	5, 47, 88
Caldwell	39
Caldwell, Rev. James	104, 106
Camden	24
Camden County	23
Campbell, Lord Neill	6, 94
Camp Middlebrook	95
Cape May	4, 29
Cape May City	32
Cape May County	28
Cape May Court House	30
Cape May Point	32
Carney's Point	84
Carr, Sir Robert	4
Carteret, Lady Elizabeth	99

	Page
Carteret, Sir George	4, 6, 88
Carteret, Philip	48, 64, 67, 68
Cedar Creek Bridge	82
Cedarville	37
Chatham	76
Chestnut Neck	10, 11
Clark, Abraham	106
Clarksboro	45
Clinton, Sir Henry	69, 70
Closter	14
Cohansey Bridge	34
Cold Spring	31
Columbia	55
Connecticut Farms	104
Cooper, J. Fenimore	16
Cooper, William	24
Cornbury, Lord	6
Cornwallis, Lord, 44, 45, 47, 48, 54, 95	
Coxe, Samuel	29, 30
Coxehall	32
Cranbury	68
Crosswicks	20
Cumberland County	33
Daretown	86
Dayton, Jonathan	102
Decatur, Stephen	42
Deerfield	36
Denning, William	22
Dennisville	30
DeVries, David Peterson	28
Dey, Colonel Theunis	82, 83
Dickinson, Philemon	57, 59
Dividing Creek	37
Donop, Count	44
Edwards, Jonathan	103
Egg Harbor	82
Elfsborg, Fort	4, 84, 88
Elizabeth	99, 100, 101, 104
Englishtown	73
Essex County	11, 38
Fairton	36
Fenwick Grove	84
Fenwick, John	5, 33, 84, 88
Finderne	94
Finn's Point	84
Fishing Creek	33
Fitch, John	57
Flatbrookville	99
Flemington	55
Forman, General David	73
Fort Elfsborg	4, 84, 88
Fort Lee	12
Fort Mercer	43
Fort Washington	12
Fox, George	74
Francis, Tench	47
Franklin, Benjamin	66

INDEX

Page

Franklin, William,
      6, 18, 64, 65, 66, 96
Freehold 69
Frelinghuysen, Frederick 92
Freneau 73
Freneau, Philip 73
Friesburg 84

Gardner, Thomas 17
Girard, Stephen 22
Glassboro 47
Gloucester County 43
Godyn 4, 28
Gravelly Point 74
Green Village 80
Greene, Colonel Christopher 43
Greene, General Nathaniel... 12, 51
Greenville 53
Greenwich 34, 37

Hackensack 13
Hackettstown 107
Haddon, Elizabeth 25, 28
Haddonfield 25
Halleck, Fitz-Greene 52
Hamburg 97
Hamilton, Alexander 53, 77, 82
Hancock's Bridge 87
Hancock, William 87, 88
Hanover 81
Harrison, William Henry........104
Hart, John 55
Harte, Bret 106
Heath, George 74
Hibernia 81
Hoboken 4, 51
Hohokus 13
Hope 107
Hopkinson, Francis 20
Howe, Lord 54, 66,106
Huddy, Captain Joshua 74, 82
Hudson County 12, 48
Hudson, Henry 10, 28
Hunter, Robert 6, 54, 64
Hunterdon County 54

Irving, Washington 42, 51, 52

Jacksonville 19
Jay, John 104
Jennings, Samuel 6, 16, 17
Jersey City 49

Kaighn, John 24, 25
Keith, George 72
Kent, Ship 5

Lafayette.. 49, 57, 76, 93, 102, 103
Lambertville 54
Lawrence, Captain James..16, 45, 65
Lawrenceville 59

Page

Lawrie, Gawen 5, 6
Lee, General Charles 70, 91
Lee, Fort 12
Lee, Harry (Light Horse) 51
Leslie, Captain William......... 92
Little Egg Harbor 5
Little Falls 83
Livingston, William 6, 104
Loantaka Valley 81
Lovelace, John Lord 6
Lucas 5

Madison 75
Mantua 47
Marlboro 73
Matawan 74
Mawhood, Colonel Charles,
      47, 87, 88
Mays Landing 10
McLane, Allen 51
Mendham 80
Mercer County 55
Mercer, General 51
Mey, Cornelius Jacobsen .. 4, 28, 44
Middlesex County 11, 63
Middletown 73
Millstone 94
Millville 38
Minnisink 98
Minuit, Peter 4
Monmouth County 11, 69
Montclair 42
Montgomerie, John 6
Moorestown 20
Morgan, Colonel Daniel 72
Morris County 75
Morris, Lewis 6, 69
Morristown 77
Morse, Samuel 80
Mount Holly 22
Mt. Vernon 80
Newark 38, 39
New Barbadoes 12
Newbie, Mark 25
New Brunswick 66
New England Town 29, 33
New Haven 4
Newton 97
North Woodbury 45

Ocean County 81
Odell, Jonathan, Rev. 16, 18
Orange 42
Oxford 107

Passaic County 12, 82
Paterson 82
Paterson, William 67, 94
Paulus Hook 4, 49
Pedricktown 84

INDEX

Page

Penn, William 5, 43
Pennington 55
Penns Neck 84
Perth Amboy 64
Pilesgrove 84
Pitcher, Molly 70
Pittsgrove 86
Plainfield 106
Pleasant Mills 10
Pluckemin 91
Pompton Lakes 82
Poor, Enoch, General.......... 14
Porch's Mill 46
Preakness 82
Princeton 59
Princeton College 24
Printz, Governor 84
Provost 13
Pulaski, Count 10, 11

Quinton's Bridge 87

Rahl, Colonel 57
Rahway 104
Ramapo 88
Revel, Thomas 17
Ringoes 54, 55
Roadstown 38
Rocky Hill 95
Rudyard 6

Salem 5, 88
Salem County 84
Schellingers Landing 32
Scott, Winfield 102
Seaville 31
Shield, Ship 6, 18
Shiloh 38
Ship Kent 5
Shrewsbury 74
Singac 83
Smith, Samuel 18
Somers Point 10, 11
Somers, Richard 11
Somerset County 90
Somerville 92

Page

South Bound Brook 95
Springfield 106
Steuben, Baron 95
Stevens, John 51, 52
Stirling, Lord 51, 91, 102
Stockton, Richard 63
Stuyvesant, Peter 4, 48
Sussex County 96
Swartwout's Pond 98
Swedesboro 45

Tennent, Rev. William 70
Toms River 82
Trenton 55
Troy Hills 81

Union County 99

Van Buren, Martin 52
Verazano 4

Warren County 107
Washington's Crossing 55
Washington, Fort 12
Washington, George,
    14, 49, 54, 57, 59, 66, 68, 70, 76
        78, 80, 93, 95, 101, 106, 107
Washington's Rock 106
Wayne, General Anthony..12, 24, 75
Webster, Daniel 53
Weehawken 52
West Englewood 12
Weymouth 11
Whippany 76
Whitall, Ann 44
Whitefield, George 103
Whitman, Walt 25
Wick, Tempe 77
William IV 22, 53
Wistarburg 84
Witherspoon, John 63
Woodbridge 67
Woodbury 44
Woodstown 88
Woolman, John 22